More Praise for Smart Parents

"The *Smart Parents* blog series and what education must become. It is practical road map for any parent, g for anyone who wants to engage you own learning." Nicholas C. Donohue Mae Education Foundation

"Packed with helpful guidance from parents who are also educators... [*Smart Parents*] prepares parents for powerful and significant contributions to their children's learning." Jennifer Miller, author and illustrator of the blog *Confident Parents, Confident Kids* and contributor to NBC Universal's Parent Toolkit

"Tom Vander Ark and the team at Getting Smart have created a critical resource with compelling stories to help parents help their children navigate these educational options." Michael B. Horn, author of *Blended: Using Disruptive Innovation to Improve Schools*

"Parents want powerful learning experiences that complement the modern realities, challenges and opportunities their children face.... [*Smart Parents*] describes how parents can help their children access the best innovations that are transforming education today." Heather Staker, Founder and President, Ready to Blend

"The *Smart Parents* blog series and book illuminate the path forward so that parents can make powerful decisions for and with their children that have the potential to impact children's lives." Nina Rees, President and CEO, National Alliance for Public Charter Schools

"*Smart Parents: Parenting for Powerful Learning* provides all families—regardless of race, socioeconomic status or zip code—the tools and resources they need to be effective advocates and inspiring teachers for their kids. Successful learners need *Smart Parents* supporting and encouraging them." Patrick Riccards, Chief Communications and Strategy Officer, The Woodrow Wilson National Fellowship Foundation

"A world-class education is now within reach of every parent for every child—but parents must be informed, involved, intentional and inspirational to make it a reality for their kids. I highly recommend this book for any parent who wants to make a significant difference in the quality and impact of their child's educational experience." Curt Allen, President and CEO, Agilix Labs

"Readers, both parents and educators, will appreciate the tools to better understand how children learn and the platforms for that learning, as well as the inspirational stories on what learning can look like for different students." Max Silverman, Associate Director at the University of Washington Center for Educational Leadership

SMART PARENTS
Parenting for Powerful Learning

Bonnie Lathram | Carri Schneider | Tom Vander Ark

Published by **Getting Smart**
1600B SW Dash Point Rd #311
Federal Way, WA 98023
www.gettingsmart.com

Getting Smart is an imprint of

Eifrig Publishing LLC

PO Box 66, Lemont, PA 16851, USA
Knobelsdorffstr. 44, 14059 Berlin, Germany
www.eifrigpublishing.com

For information regarding permissions, write to:
editor@gettingsmart.com

Library of Congress Cataloging-in-Publication Data

Lathram, Bonnie, Carri Schneider and Tom Vander Ark
    Smart Parents: Parenting for Powerful Learning /
by Bonnie Lathram, Carri Schneider and Tom Vander Ark

p.   cm.

Paperback: ISBN 978-1-63233-066-6
Ebook: ISBN 978-1-63233-067-3

1. Education 2. Parenting 3. Schools and Teaching
    I. Lathram, Bonnie, Carri Schneider and Tom Vander Ark,
    II. Title.

20 19 18 17 2016
5   4   3   2   1

Printed on acid-free paper. ∞

TABLE OF CONTENTS

Preface

Everything is Different Now: Parenting for Powerful Learning
Tom Vander Ark

"When our daughter was born 30 years ago, the primary educational duties for parents were reading to your kid and making sure she got into a good school. There was a high level of trust and respect for authorities; we assumed that schools would prepare students for their future. My first indication that this simple formula might not work out was when my older daughter rebelled at her obedience-focused, traditional school with desks in rows.

Twenty years ago, the Internet exploded, and my daughter's fifth-grade teacher understood the profound shift to information abundance. He used technology to drive student-centered, inquiry-based learning. His classroom, and thousands like his, launched the learning revolution. Ten years ago, tablet computers were introduced, app stores erupted, and inexpensive mobile technology began closing the digital divide. And now, the first generation of young people, including my daughter, raised on cell phones and the Oregon Trail are giving birth to children who will benefit from thinking machines and personalized pathways. The good news is that we're the first generation with a shot at offering every young person on the planet a great education. The bad news is that we don't have a framework for being parents and teachers in this new age."

Pause for a minute, and consider some of the innovations introduced in the last 30 years that impact the way you experience the world on a daily basis: the Internet, email, smartphones, ATMs, flat-panel displays, GPS devices and social networks. A quick scan of your day so far will give lots of evidence that the world has significantly changed since your parents were your age. We all know the world is rapidly shifting, but we're just beginning to understand what this all means for kids who are coming of age in the Digital Era.

Tom's daughters, now 26 and 30, were among the first generation to benefit from computer learning games, cell phones and the ability to build a high school transcript that included online and college courses. Fifteen years later, educational options have expanded dramatically for most families, requiring daily decisions about the modular learning landscape.

When Bonnie began teaching high school in the early 2000s, students had mobile devices for texting and phone calls, but no "smart" capabilities. The class rule back then dictated that cell phones stayed out of sight. However, in more recent years, when Bonnie taught high school seniors, most of her students had Internet-connected devices and constant online access throughout the day. Many of her high school students used their phones for school work—taking notes, getting in touch with mentors, looking for directions to get to internships and working on college essays via Google Docs.

When Carri was a second grader in the 1980s, being "tech-savvy" meant successfully loading the Oregon Trail floppy disk by herself, without interrupting the teacher. Now her "tech-savvy" second-grade daughter can create and deliver Google presentations with embedded videos, is learning to code and regularly emails her friends.

We live in an era of extraordinary learning opportunities.

Today's students can look up why Gandhi led a hunger strike or how the early civil rights movement spurred the anti-war movement of the late 1960s—all from their devices. Students can connect virtually with mentors and experts to bring learning to life. Students can watch demonstration videos on Khan Academy and YouTube to learn how molecules split or how to divide polynomials. The ability to Internet search, the most important learning tool ever invented, is now being replaced by smart algorithms that push information our direction, as we need it. Students have begun to benefit from unique playlists of learning experiences driven by a recommendation engine.[2]

As educators and as parents, we have seen profound shifts in the way that human beings learn—those of us young and old. Formal and informal learning options have exploded. Students can now learn anywhere, and at anytime. Yet, the levels of underemployment and debt among young adults suggest that the old trajectory of "do well, go to college, get a job" is broken. The opportunity set has never been greater, and the challenges have never been more complex. Families face unprecedented amounts of information and education-related decisions. This often leaves parents navigating a complex maze of new learning opportunities, new standards, new assessments and new technology.

The Smart Parents project grew out of the recognition that parents need help making informed decisions, finding quality resources and providing the best supports for their children. The project, hatched around the office kitchen counter in the summer of 2014, began as a blog series by and about parents advocating for powerful learning. With the support of the Nellie Mae Education Foundation, we cultivated more than 60 parent contributions about how to recognize, create and advocate for powerful, student-centered learning opportunities.

At Getting Smart, our Seattle-based learning design firm, we study innovations in learning. We spend a lot of our time creating and sharing resources for teachers, leaders, policymakers and education organizations. Time and time again, we observe that families get left out of the equation when it comes to determining the primary audience for education reports, papers and articles—even though they are among the hungriest for informed opinions that can help them. We aim to change that.

This book by parents and for parents intends to be a guide to powerful personalized learning. Don't expect a general guidebook on parenting; you can find hundreds of those at the library. This book was designed to facilitate important educational decisions that parents face today. Numerous paths exist toward powerful, student-centered learning; this project focuses on innovations in teaching and learning that boost engagement, activate interests, extend access and personalize learning.

Given the drastic ways in which the world is rapidly changing, you may be curious—like us—about how these changes impact the ways that we teach our young people and the ways young people now learn. Parenting for powerful learning revolves around being informed, inspirational, intentional and involved. Have you been thinking about these questions:

- How you can advocate for your child's individual needs as a learner?

- How are schools changing to meet the needs of all learners?

- What shifts are happening at your child's school or in your child's learning as a result of technology, and what do you need to know to support your child?

- What's the meaning behind new terms like "blended learning" and "flipped learning"? (In Appendix C, we provide a handy glossary for a host of education terms!)

Maybe you're here to seek information and inspiration so that you can approach your child's education differently. This book is for parents and guardians like you. We hope it will also prove useful for teachers, school and district leaders, and tutors and youth service providers, as well as any organization whose mission involves improving access and outcomes for students.

The three authors have a combined six decades of experience in education. Among us, there's a former superintendent, a former high school teacher and a former elementary school teacher-turned-college professor. We are also parents. Our children range from infants to adults. We represent a wide range of parenthood; one of us is balancing the sleepless nights of infanthood, one is navigating elementary school-based decisions, and the other is transitioning from being a parent to also a grandparent.

Why an Anti-Screen Family Has Gone Blended
Heather Staker

"Two components—the personalized, online learning blended with the collaborative, offline inquiry—are the promise of the next generation of schooling. For too long, schools have been stressed with trying to deliver a standardized, comprehensive education in an inflexible model. Little time is left either for personal adaptation or for deep inquiry. The best blended-learning implementations are breaking the rules of that model and discovering newfound possibilities. The acquisition of core skills is becoming personalized, adaptive and student-driven. This in turn is freeing up time and capacity to attend to higher forms of reasoning and development throughout the rest of the day. That blend has sharpened the intellectual, moral and interpersonal development of our children. We have found it hard to turn back."[3]

What Kids Should Know and Be Able to Do

As parents and educators, we've come to understand that every child has unique strengths and challenges. We believe young people should have the opportunity to learn in the best ways possible for them. We believe young people learn best by doing and, to the extent possible, driving their own learning. There is, however, a standard body of knowledge, set of skills and range of dispositions that generally prove useful in successfully mastering self-expression, employment and overall citizenship. It is the artful way—often called student-centered learning—in which parents and teachers create, combine and encourage learning experiences to leverage interest and cultivate critical skills and mindsets. We believe new student-centered learning tools and strategies represent an unprecedented global learning opportunity.

Traditional education pushes students with similar birthdays through a common curriculum that focuses on memorizing facts and procedures. The most compliant and well-supported young people are able to pass college entrance exams, but formal education leaves many unprepared to thrive in the world they will inherit.

We live in a world that is increasingly complex. It's connected but segmented into narrow channels. It's hypercompetitive but emphasizes collaboration. It values unique and creative contributions. This suggests new priorities for what young people need to know and be able to do. The Partnership for 21st Century Skills summarizes key skills as four Cs: critical thinking, communication, collaboration and creativity.[4]

 Good Work

Just doing well in school isn't good enough anymore; it's a goal too narrow to inspire and too inadequate to prepare. In Five Minds for the Future, Howard Gardner suggests young people should have the opportunity to develop a disciplined, creative, respectful and ethical mind capable of synthesizing information for productive purposes. He suggests aiming for "good work"—work that is excellent, ethical and engaging. (We agree and run a regular blog series on Good Work.) Most importantly, Gardner suggests that parents should model good work, meaning young people should witness pride and ethical behavior from parents as they engage in work and service.

College-bound aspirations are great, but the character that young people develop proves most important to their success in life. Business leaders say work ethic is the number one thing they look for. Paul Tough, author of "How Children Succeed: Grit, Curiosity and the Hidden Power of Character," says, "We don't teach the most important skills." His list includes "persistence, self-control, curiosity, conscientiousness, grit and self-confidence."

Embracing a broader set of learning goals may seem daunting to parents and teachers, but what young people learn is not separate from who they become. It is the learning experiences created by—and support provided by—parents and teachers that shape young people's knowledge, skills and dispositions.

Encouraging Non-Conformity

Investor Peter Thiel thinks we could encourage nonconformity. In hiring and investing, he looks for "Zen-like opposites: people that are really stubborn and really open-minded." He wants people who are really idiosyncratic but work well in teams. Thiel suggests, "If you focus on one end or the other, you get it wrong; it's the combination of unusual traits that produces interesting ideas." On daring to be different, Thiel says, "Brilliant thinking is rare, but courage is in even shorter supply than genius."[5]

As we discuss further in Chapter One, parents who convey and model the enjoyment of learning for learning's sake (not just asking their children about grades received on a test) help to cultivate the mindsets, skills and dispositions that researchers have begun to understand in deeper ways as a key differentiator in success, as measured by college graduation rates and subsequent career satisfaction.

Students need to have content knowledge to be successful in college, and they also need a broader set of skills and conditions including: the ability to set short- and long-term goals; leadership experience; community involvement and internships; perseverance through challenges; a positive self-concept about learning as well as a realistic sense of academic and personal strengths and growth areas.[6]

Four Keys to Parenting For Powerful Learning. As educators, we appreciate the importance of common expectations rooted in research and our shared reality. As parents, we appreciate that every young person is unique. Our main job revolves around cultivating the remarkable gifts of each child and encouraging him or her to discover and explore individual passions and purpose. This is even more important than any external definition or measure of college readiness.

From our long-term, informal study of parenting for powerful learning, we have observed that Smart Parents are:

- involved in their children's lives,
- informed about and advocates for their children's learning,
- intentional about creating powerful learning experiences, and
- inspirational as learning guides and role models.

The parents' perspectives, tips and tools mentioned throughout this book illustrate these four characteristics.

Using This Book

The book is organized into two parts. **Part One** describes the current opportunities and challenges encountered by parents and students. We focus on the individual uniqueness of each child, the exploding set of options for learning, and the role that technology plays in the process. We explore student-centered learning, the question of why it's so important, and actions you can take to cultivate this at home, at school and everywhere else. **Part Two** offers a Smart Parent Toolkit full of resources to help you put these ideas into practice.

In each chapter, you'll find icons that indicate features in the book. Because parents have created this book for parents, we feature an abundance of parent-centric stories. Each links back to the original, full blog post online. That means if you are reading this digitally, you can read more by simply clicking on the link. If you are reading this in print, you can find each blog on our GettingSmart.com and Huffington Post Smart Parents sites; we hope you read on to delve deeper! The stories have been so inspiring and have become some of our favorite parts of this book.

Icon Key

To help readers navigate the chapters and make the most of the information, there are chapter and sidebar icons (introduced on the next page) to help denote features of the book:

The "parent perspective" icon marks a short story at the beginning of each chapter and blog-length parent stories at the end of each chapter.

 The "school spotlight" icon denotes schools that exemplify student-centered learning in action.

 The "toolkit" icon indicates a particular resource, actionable tip or strategy. Even more tools, tips and strategies can be found in Part Two of this book—the <u>Smart Parent Toolkit</u>.

 The "informed" icon denotes a story or tool that provides more information for parents.

 The "involved" icon marks a tool, tip or strategy for parents to promote student-centered learning.

 The "intentional" icon illustrates ways parents can focus attention on student-centered learning.

 The "inspirational" icon illustrates pathways for parents that will encourage them to both model and inspire their children in learning.

Parent Perspectives

Throughout each chapter of this book, we feature parent stories written by parents, for parents, that originally appeared as feature blogs on our Smart Parents channel on GettingSmart.com and on our Smart Parents partner site on The Huffington Post. These stories illustrate real examples of those who parent for powerful learning—inside and outside of the classroom.

Acknowledgements

We approach the topic of parenting with humility—and openness to learning. We drew on the experience of our spouses, colleagues, partners and more than 60 national experts and parents. We appreciate the hard work put in by all parents and adults who help to teach our children—all those parents, guardians, grandparents, relatives, teachers, mentors, coaches and caring adults who work to make the lives of young people better.

The authors wish to thank the many contributors who engaged with us over social media and through blog contributions, comments on our site, conversations and interviews over the last year. A list of the blog contributions of more than 60 parents is in Appendix B with links to the full blog posts. These stories formed the foundation and inspiration for this book.

The Nellie Mae Education Foundation made this project possible. We appreciate Nicholas Donohue's leadership on student-centered learning.

We also wish to thank and acknowledge our own "smart parents" who taught and modeled the value of lifelong learning. To this day, our parents continue to encourage and inspire our work.

This was a full team effort by the Getting Smart crew. Mary Ryerse provided early inspiration and Caroline Vander Ark modeled the way. We had many ongoing conversations during the last year about the Getting Smart team members' individual experiences as parents, sons and daughters. Smart Team, we sincerely could not have done it without you.

Thank you to Corinne Whiting for copy editing, Kelley Tanner for her design work, Liz Wimmer for her research support and proofreading and Penelope Eifrig for publishing support.

Thanks to our spouses for their love and support. Writing a book is a bit like having another child. It requires time, attention and a lot of nurturing. Thanks for putting up with us as we spent many nights researching, writing and editing this book.

Finally, we dedicate this book to our own children (and grandchildren), who challenge and inspire us to be Smart Parents every day.

Introduction
By Nicholas Donohue

Our education system was designed for an era that no longer exists. Our world is changing rapidly, and this has profound implications for how our young people learn. Formal and informal learning options abound. As opportunities and options explode, families face unprecedented amounts of decisions related to education.

As parents, we know now that a high school diploma is no longer an indicator of future success. Today's students must leave high school prepared for success in post-secondary schooling or training. Our students must also be equipped with skills such as creativity, communication, critical thinking and collaboration—new basics, if you will, for a modern age.

My own daughters are very successful in the traditional system, but I share concerns with other parents about how they are being challenged to exercise their minds and grow the real, practical skills needed to succeed. One approach being promoted nationally to address these concerns involves renovating our education system to deliver student-centered approaches to learning, sometimes known more simply as personalized learning. These approaches, built on research and the science of learning, are aimed at elevating outcomes and broadening the fit of public education with a wider variety of learners and a wider variety of preferences, strengths and needs.

What is Student-Centered Learning? For starters, we envision an education system where learning transcends the traditional school calendar and setting. We envision a system where student progress is based on mastery of a skill or topic, rather than time spent in a classroom—one that is feasibly customized in practical, cost-effective ways that garner results strong enough to predict future success in life and work.

Student-Centered Learning
tinyurl.com/VIDEO-SCL

We know parents play a huge role in implementing the principles of student-centered learning—learning that is personalized, engaging, competency-based and can happen anytime, anywhere.

Student-centered learning engages students in their own success—and incorporates their interests and skills in the learning process. Rather than responding to educators who hand down information, students can engage with teachers and their peers in real-time—preparing them to succeed in college and future careers. Beyond college and career readiness, a real desire exists to prepare our young people to be lifelong learners. This means not only thinking about whether they can enter the 21st-century economy, but also whether they love to learn, feel empathy toward others, and care for the planet.

What are Student-Centered Approaches? Student-centered approaches to learning highlight four key tenets (further described below), drawn from the mind/brain sciences, learning theory and research on youth development that prove essential to students' full engagement in achieving Deeper Learning outcomes.

 Student-Centered Learning

- is personalized
- is competency-based
- happens anytime, anywhere
- encourages students to take ownership over their own learning

Learning is Personalized. Personalized learning recognizes that students engage in different ways and in different places. As parent Christine Byrd describes in Chapter Three in this book, "Volunteering in [my son's] class, I was blown away by the range of skills these 5-year-olds brought. Some were reading books and writing in complete sentences before the first day, while others were still learning the alphabet. How could any teacher manage such disparity in her daily lessons, much less challenge the advanced kids while nurturing those who needed some extra help? Obviously this is where 'self-paced' and 'individualized' learning get their appeal." Students benefit from individually paced, targeted learning tasks that start from the student's current position, formatively assess existing skills and knowledge as well as address the student's needs and interests.

Learning is Competency-Based. Students move ahead when they have demonstrated mastery of content, not when they've reached a certain birthday or completed the required hours in a classroom. When describing her daughter's efforts to master math content, mother Sarah Vander Schaaff writes in Chapter Three about what you can do to ensure your child can move at his or her own pace.

Learning Happens Anytime, Anywhere. Learning takes place beyond the traditional school day—and even beyond the school year. The school's walls are permeable; learning should not be restricted to the classroom. To enhance his son's learning and activate pre-existing interests, in Chapter Five, Michael Harlow describes taking his son John to the aquarium, museums and the MakerSpace at his local library, plus taking advantage of online opportunities such as the NASA website and Minecraft.

Students Take Ownership over Their Learning. Student-centered learning engages students in their own success—and incorporates their interests and skills in the learning process. As mother Antonia Slagle writes in Chapter Two, "My son and I agree that one of the most powerful feelings in the world is the 'I did this!' feeling. That only comes from true ownership. He wrote a couple of short films. He started playing electronic music. He built websites. I have a laundry list of student internships and projects that most adults can't believe a young person accomplished." Antonia adds that as part of her son's schooling experience, "Students also reflect regularly as part of the project process and have the time and space to learn from both the successes and the mistakes."

For my eighth-grader, this would mean building on her strong interests around math, but making learning opportunities more practical and real world-oriented—presenting her with real-life problems to solve, based on (but not limited to) theoretical constructs. Math is a language we can use to describe the world as much as literature, but not if it is delivered without demonstrating how to apply it practically or by making transparent how "thinking through math" enriches analytic skills necessary for many related tasks. For my 19-year-old, this could have meant balancing her 4.75 GPA-attaining habits with her love for theater so as to make the latter more central, not simply subjugating it to an elective option so separate from "regular school."

More importantly, for my children's friends for whom traditional school is much harder–young people as good, as important, and as interested in succeeding as my own children—this could mean providing more varied and appropriate chances to apply grit, to dig deep, to work hard, and to exercise skills necessary to later succeed in the real world and achieve at high levels. For many reasons, my girls were always going to succeed despite the current approaches. For many others, the deck needs to be restacked—not to make things easier or more fun, but to make them more fair and to align how we educate with what is known about students' learning needs, rather than organizing education as a one-size-fits-all endurance test with the "gold ring" reward equaling too few available seats in college programs.

We need to make this move as a society; the future of our communities, our children, our grandchildren and their neighbors depends on it. The time has passed for a 19th-century system that selects the winner. We need a 21st-century system that truly prepares learners.

One question people regularly ask me is: Given that your own children are successful in the current system, would you support their participation in a student-centered learning environment? The answer is an unqualified "yes"! I answer this way in part because I spend my working life trying to understand these approaches; I have reconciled that, while there would be costs involved, they would be worth it in the long run.

The costs include giving up class rank. My 19-year-old ranked number five out of 500 in her high school class. I liked that recognition. So did she. My 14-year-old is headed toward the same single-digit position; what parents wouldn't want the same for their daughter? But this kind of comparative accomplishment suggests that some students are better than others; however, many with lower "rankings" might also actually be ready to step forward to greater educational challenges or a more secure measure in which to reveal competency and a readiness to move forward.

Some emerging research bolsters this conclusion, suggesting that valedictorians don't necessarily fare well in college and the workplace—in part because, despite being game winners, they often have trouble thinking outside the box. This explains why colleges want "well-rounded" applicants; administrators understand that the breadth of experience, skills and knowledge cannot simply be tied to test outcomes.

My "expert" perspective is impacted by my daughter's pleas: "What's taking you so long? Fix the schools." My kids don't like the idea that, in a student-centered future, education might become more rigorous or that there might be a whole group of kids who get A's because they have mastered the material. But they do like the idea that they can "think" and be their full selves during school, as well as before and after it.

Beginning last fall, the NMEF team partnered with Getting Smart to cultivate more than 60 parent stories and to learn from experts in the field about how to recognize, create and advocate for powerful, student-centered learning opportunities. We tell parents' stories and bring together key lessons to create a resource that will help guide important educational decisions parents face today.

We believe parents play the most important role in helping to create conditions in which student-centered learning can thrive—at home, at school and everywhere in between.

We hope you find the parent stories that follow compelling and inspiring and that you will become a strong advocate for such learning. We need parents involved with schools, teachers and students—those who recognize and advocate for student-centered learning.

Part One:
Modern Learning, Modern Parenting

Chapter One highlights the roles and responsibilities of parents and students in navigating complex educational opportunities and cultivating mindsets that support learning.

Chapter Two describes how to help your learners develop plans to support lifelong learning.

Chapter Three defines competency-based learning and offers strategies for parents to ensure students move at their own pace.

Chapter Four emphasizes that learning happens anytime and anywhere and provides parents with ways to help kids find their ideal places for learning.

Chapter Five describes the importance of encouraging student ownership over learning.

Chapter 1:
Smart Parents, Smart Students

I Need a Learning Sherpa
Katherine Prince

"I think that parents need 'learning sherpas' who can help us navigate the expanding learning landscape and design learning journeys that meet our children where they are. We need expert navigators who can share insights from the journeys of those before us, tell us what pitfalls and promises to expect around the next bend and help us surface and assess learning options that best fit our children and circumstances. These learning sherpas could shoulder some of the weight and walk alongside us as we make choices for and with our children.

In today's formal learning landscape, parents could use some inside scoop about what various public schools are really like—which students they serve well, which ones they don't or whether the socio-economic pressures are insufferable. Parents could also use help comparing neighborhood schools against other options such as charter, parochial, independent and online schools. How can we compare performance across schools that use different measures of success? What kinds of learning cultures are at play? How fluid are the schools' boundaries? Which is the right school for my child at this moment in time? What if that school isn't right in two years? What if it mostly is, but [my daughter] needs additional support or wants to pursue an interest that the curriculum can't accommodate?"[7]

The first lessons in parental responsibility come pretty early—often before a child breathes his or her first breath of air. It doesn't take much longer than that first trip to the doctor's office for expecting parents to feel the weight of key decisions. Future parents leave prenatal visits loaded with lists and reminders about how to best influence the development of their future child by focusing on diet options, exercise routines, environmental factors, lifestyle choices and more.

Carri recalls coming away from her first prenatal appointment eight years ago, immediately calling her mom from the car—tearful, overwhelmed and paralyzed by all the information just thrown her way by the doctor in the form of an inch-thick packet of "do's and don'ts." By the time she was pregnant with her second child just four years later, the standard doctor packet had been supplemented with downloadable apps for tracking daily child development, weekly email reminders of "do's and don'ts," more Facebook groups about parenting than she could count and what seemed like a constant bombardment of opinionated online articles addressing every possible parenting decision from prenatal vitamins to preschools.

Carri's experience with the new volume of information available via technology provides merely one piece of evidence that our rapidly-changing world has also changed the ways in which we parent. It's also evidence that more information doesn't necessarily mean better information.

As Katherine's reflection on choosing a preschool for her 3-year-old daughter illustrates, today's parents face an unprecedented amount of information; yet they still often lack the detailed guidance needed to make the best educational decisions for their children. Her story, like so many others, exemplifies a modern parenting paradox that leaves many feeling overwhelmed by—and underprepared for—the complex (and often high-stakes) decisions that affect the current and future well-being of our children.

 Looking for a Second Opinion

As Solomon Steplight, CEO of <u>Prepfoleo</u> (a website where parents, students and professionals can curate and crowdsource educational resources), writes, "Traditionally, parents relied on school to give their students an education. But teachers and administrators alike have encouraged parents to get more involved. Parents have more choices than ever, and they are increasingly turning to each other and the Internet for information on how to process those choices. Call it looking for a second opinion."[8]

From playground conversations to reports in the national media, both anecdotal and research-based evidence exists that confirms that modern-day parents feel confused and conflicted about everything from screen time to school choice and "opting out" of state tests to "opting in" to traditional college paths. Parents turn to social media, take advice from parent bloggers, ask their friends and neighbors and, in some cases, even hire education consultants to help them weigh school options.[9]

As Bill Jackson, founder and CEO of <u>GreatSchools,</u> writes in <u>Parental Perfection, Reimagined,</u> "More than ever before, parents in America are facing enormous pressure to be perfect. The spread of social networks has made it easy to observe fellow parents and instantly feel doubtful or inadequate about one's own beliefs and direction. Between scheduling well-rounded extracurricular activities, moderating screen time or enforcing dietary boundaries, it's not unusual to worry about taking the wrong approach. The same concerned feeling often pops up when parents make decisions regarding their child's education. GreatSchools is on a mission to debunk the perfect parent myth and instead foster the informed parent. Parents and guardians who have access to information, particularly when it comes to a child's education, can make smarter choices as they pave the way for a bright future."[10]

Parental Perfection, Reimagined
Bill Jackson

"Informed parents are more proactive about getting the facts in an efficient, effective manner. There are three habits of informed parents that we've noticed over the years:

Talk regularly with your child's teacher and principal. Fortunately, new technology now makes it possible for parents to have a direct line with educators. Apps like ClassDojo and Remind facilitate frequent communication between parents and teachers, so everyone can be open about the issues kids might be facing at school.

Ask your child one question about what they learned every day. There's an important distinction here: Don't just ask them what they learned; go a step further, and ask them to tell you more about the subject, topic or lesson. More qualitative questions can often prompt more informative answers."

Teach yourself. Recent confusion aroun...
State Standards has been a challenge for ...
formed parents. GreatSchools created Miles...
collection of online videos, so parents could te...
selves what success looks like in in grades K-5. ...
in English or Spanish, each short clip shows what st...
should be able to demonstrate by the end of the yea... to
achieve grade-level standards in critical skills like reading,
writing and math. The videos help parents answer the universal question, "Is my child on track in school?"

By keeping these three tactics in mind, parents are
better able to support their children's learning at home
and advocate for their children at school. They can feel
more confident in their understanding of where their
children stand and whether they are on track for college.
By parenting smarter, not harder, they can be informed,
which as it turns out, is much easier than being perfect."[11]

Broader Aims

The backdrop of our increasingly digital lives carries great
importance, but it's not the whole story. There is much to
consider at the intersection of parenting and technology—
from educational videos for infants to issues facing personal
online security for middle schoolers and concerns over digital reputations for high school graduates. But it's about more
than making sure that our kids are safe or that they're not
spending too much time playing video games. Parenting in
the Digital Era also involves understanding the educational
opportunities available to our kids, so we can help them
harness the power of these opportunities. A national, online
survey of parents of kids in grades 3 through 12, "Parents'
Attitudes Toward Educational Technology," found that
the majority of parents feel good about the growing use of

...nology in education, and most think it is improving the quality of their children's education.[12]

We believe in the potential of technology to improve student access and extend learning opportunities, but parenting for powerful learning is not about plugging your kids into technology and proudly declaring victory over the shifting realities of the 21st century. The real point of parenting for powerful learning means that parents play a critical role in helping their children navigate the myriad formal and informal options that are available to them, helping to equip them with the habits and mindsets necessary to drive their own learning. Doing so demands recognizing the shifts in how, when, where and even why we learn. And that recognition comes from the acknowledgement of an alarming and widespread problem: The current education system is in need of an update.

Defining Education

We define "education" as more than core content subjects and mastery of content and skills measured by traditional metrics like one's GPA and SAT scores. Education is the formal and informal learning experiences that form the knowledge, skills and dispositions necessary for success in careers and citizenship. More broadly, as Harvard professor and author Howard Gardner says, "Education is inherently and inevitably an issue of human goals and human values."[13] However, finding a common way to discuss and embrace these broader aims can be challenging. We refer to these aspirations as "next generation" (next-gen) education. Widely recognized frameworks are discussed below and further defined in the glossary found within Appendix C.

The United States Department of Education has weighed in on what parents should expect from their children's education. In June 2015, U.S. Education Secretary Arne Duncan released a set of parental rights designed to help prepare every student for success in life.[14] The rights outline what families should expect. The rights include free, quality preschool; high, challenging standards and engaging teaching and leadership in a safe, supportive, well resourced school; and an affordable, quality college degree.

These rights are unlikely to fuel debates from parent advocates, but it's unclear how these rights will be enacted and what they mean for reimagining the educational experiences of America's young people. From the implementation of Common Core State Standards to the parental pushback on week-long, high-stakes testing, a national conversation has begun that highlights the need to transform the education system. However, that debate is often limited to the politics and policies of education, not the actual learner experiences likely to produce lifelong benefits.

A generation ago, if your child was accepted into college, he or she could probably graduate and find a job in a relevant field. But these days, it's not just about grades, SAT scores and college admissions; the level of young adult underemployment and debt suggests that the high school (or even college) diploma no longer guarantees a living wage. We know far too many students who have been able to navigate the system and call the value of school into question, even having already earned their degree. We've also known far too many students who suffer from lack of engagement and leave college with high debt—and no degree. In both cases, there seem to be missed opportunities with serious implications.

The young adult unemployment rate has consistently been higher than the overall rate for adults, but the Great Recession proved particularly bad for young workers, with unemployment spiking to more than 16 percent. By March 2015, overall unemployment was down to 5.5 percent, but it remained at 7.8 percent for workers aged 18 to 34—and nearly twice that for African Americans.[15] Combine this with the high rate of student debt, and one can obtain a clearer picture of the financial realities young people face. The class of 2013 graduates left college with an average debt approaching $30,000.[16]

As Tatyana Warrick of the Partnership for 21st-Century Learning writes, "As our world of work and learning becomes more complex, so does parenting and the importance of supporting 21st-century learning for even the earliest learners. Students today need to be globally aware and competent, digitally savvy, engaged as 21st-century citizens and able to master content deeply, in order to not only ace end-of-year tests but also big tests that come later like that first college application and first "real" job. The skills they will need involve the 4 C's—Communication, Collaboration, Critical Thinking and Creativity, which are often cited as 21st-century skills. However, in a newer twist, they prove so important for all kids, not just those lucky enough to live in the right zip code. These skills foster thinking outside the box and they drive innovation—both for our economy and our society."[17]

Embrace Broader Goals

Helping your son or daughter embrace broader learning goals requires conversations about experiences and academic work. Assembling a digital portfolio of artifacts can be a good way for youth to track their growth on broader aims and broader measures—beyond bubble tests and the number of college acceptance letters received.

Ted Dintersmith, producer of the documentary film "Most Likely to Succeed," shines a light on the need for a modern update to public education through an evocative look at new school models that hold promise. He explains, "What I find shocking is that schools aren't preparing our kids for life in the 21st century. Surrounded by innovation, our education system is stuck in the 19th century. The skills and capabilities our kids need going forward are either ignored or outright trampled."[18]

involved

3 Factors to Consider When Choosing an Innovative School
Nina Rees

"Given the variety of options and innovations out there, what should parents look for when choosing the best school for their child? As a mom and a leader in the charter school movement, I'd consider the following three factors.

First, take a close look at school culture and mission. While it may be harder to gauge than more concrete metrics like students per teacher or achievement test scores, culture goes a long way in determining how schools operate. For instance, if a school says its goal is to get every student ready for college, how is it innovating to reach that goal?

Second, ask about the school's technology priorities, and how those priorities shape its work. While just about every school uses technology to some extent—and some programs and platforms are ubiquitous—does any school not incorporate Khan Academy lessons at this point? Each school will emphasize investments in certain areas that coincide with other pedagogical goals.

Third, find out how a school's view of innovation goes beyond technology. In many schools, it's common to give students their own Chromebooks and iPads and to provide access to the latest educational software and apps. Yet it's just as important to determine how technology makes other innovative learning goals achievable."[19]

As parents, we know intuitively that are involvement in the lives of our kids matters. And yet, parent advocacy looks different depending on who you talk to. So, what does advocacy look like from the perspective of real parents? We explore parental advocacy in greater detail in Chapter Two.

Teachers, Parents and Students: Relationship-Rich Environment Promotes Learning

Michael Levine, the founding director of the Joan Ganz Cooney Center at Sesame Workshop, describes the impact of families on learning, "Research on young children's developing brains and self-regulation as active learners is now aligned with decades of research by experts on school climate and parent engagement. Dr. Daniel Siegel, a pioneering neuropsychiatrist at UCLA, recently observed: 'Studies of longevity, medical and mental health, happiness and even wisdom point to relationships as the most robust predictor of positive attributes in our lives across the lifespan.'

These insights align with what pioneers such as Dr. James Comer of Yale University pointed out more than two decades ago. The power of school can be enhanced or diminished by the types of relationships that are formed at the core of our educational enterprise. Teachers, parents, supervisors and students must be linked together in a relationship-rich environment that is open, flexible and relentlessly promotes learning."[20]

As the face of American public education slowly evolves from a factory-model system to a modern-era system, parents can inform what students should know and be able to do as they advance from "cradle to career." Beyond choosing optimal educational options, parents can stay ahead by understanding which habits, skills and mindsets support their students and how they can help cultivate them.

Habits and Mindsets Matter

One of the most exciting developments in education involves a growing recognition of "growth mindsets." A growth mindset is the belief or understanding that intelligence can be developed. Students with a growth mindset focus on improvement instead of worrying about their intelligence level. They work hard to learn more and get smarter. Researchers have found that having a growth mindset proves really important for success in school. Eduardo Briceño, co-founder of Mindset Works, an organization that works to promote growth mindset in students, says, "People who believe that leadership skills are developed–a growth mindset about leadership skills–feel inspired rather than threatened by other leaders, have higher confidence in their own ability to lead, and experience lower anxiety and higher performance in leadership activities. Managers who believe that personal qualities can change, seek and welcome feedback more, notice changes in employee performance more accurately, and take on more coaching-oriented behaviors, leading to improved team capability and performance. And lots of research has shown that children with a growth mindset seek more effective learning strategies, work harder, persevere in the face of setbacks and achieve higher competence."[21]

Activating Growth Mindsets

Parents can encourage a growth mindset by praising effort over product. For example, let's imagine your student did really well on a math quiz. Instead of saying, "You are so smart. You are really great at math," try, "I can tell how hard you worked on this. You put a lot of effort into learning your math concepts. I'm proud of you."

In a related New York magazine article, "How Not To Talk To Your Kids" by Po Bronson, the author offers this example about encouraging a growth mindset through conversations with his son Luke:

"I tried to use the specific-type praise that [Stanford University researcher Carol] Dweck recommends. I praised Luke, but I attempted to praise his 'process.' This was easier said than done. What are the processes that go on in a 5-year-old's mind? In my impression, 80 percent of his brain processes lengthy scenarios for his action figures.

But every night he has math homework and is supposed to read a phonics book aloud. Each takes about five minutes if he concentrates, but he's easily distracted. So I praised him for concentrating without asking to take a break. If he listened to instructions carefully, I praised him for that. After soccer games, I praised him for looking to pass, rather than just saying, 'You played great.' And if he worked hard to get to the ball, I praised the effort he applied. Just as the research promised, this focused praise helped him see strategies he could apply the next day. It was remarkable how noticeably effective this new form of praise was."[22]

As parents, we are our children's first teachers, and children learn by watching what we model. These mindsets and habits include persistence, effort, self-control, curiosity, creativity and self-confidence. In front of our children, how we model our own ability to persevere, set goals, work through challenges and continue to try, despite failure or success, proves critical. Parents who praise work ethic rather than fixed intelligence help to encourage a child's positive self-confidence and innate beliefs about him or herself as a learner.

Arina Bokas, Clarkson PTA President, and Rod Rock, superintendent of Clarkston Community Schools in Clarkston, Michigan, writes in Changing the Mindset of Education: Every Learner is Unique that there is a strong need for schools to understand the importance of activating and encouraging growth mindsets: "Imagine a student who hears things once and knows them forever. She is a good reader. She is self-aware and can articulate her learning challenges and successes. Despite the fact that the student is smart, she struggles on written work and in group projects. How does our school system help encourage a student with her potential and her challenges? ... In a growth-mindset system that is focused on strengths, aptitudes and individual differences in children, we would refer to a child as mathematically, intra-personal, or linguistically intelligent. We would notice each child's natural proclivities and strengths, and we would use this knowledge to help individual children learn math, science, social studies, art, music and communication skills in ways that work best for each one of them. Each child is unique and uniquely smart, as parents know. We must expect and require our school systems to figure out how and to help each child to use his or her smarts to live a happy life and to achieve at the highest levels possible."[23]

**Parent Resources for
Activating a Growth Mindset**

If you're interested in learning more, see <u>Collaborative for Academic, Social, and Emotional Learning, Edutopia and Mindset Works</u>. For more specific strategies on social and emotional development and growth mindset, see the <u>Smart Parent Toolkit</u>.

A 2015 report titled "<u>Foundations for Young Adult Success: A Developmental Framework</u>" has identified a definition of success that both encompasses workforce goals around college and career readiness and also identifies broader goals for learning: "While building an educated workforce is one of the core goals of our investments in young people, it is far from the only goal. Success also means that young people can fulfill individual goals and have the agency and competencies to influence the world around them. This broader definition of success is based on the synthesis of literature from various fields, as well as interviews with practice experts and youth service providers, who articulated their larger role as helping young people develop an awareness of themselves and of the wide range of options before them, competencies to pursue those options and the ability to make good future choices for their lives as engaged citizens in the world. This larger focus is inseparable from goals related to college and career."[24]

We think it's important for parents to keep in mind that, although our culture tends to reward success as a "good job" or attendance at a "good college," in our hearts, parents understand that success is broader and more nuanced. In fact, we heard this over and over in our Smart Parents blog series as well. Inspiring lifelong learning and cultivating joy, curiosity and happiness are related to college and career success and prove to be all-encompassing goals.

We seek to provide a lens for parents to see how a few academics and organizations—education experts and researchers—define the knowledge, skills and dispositions or mindsets that impact college and career success and inspire lifelong learning.

We share this context to give parents a peek into the complexity of various attempts to define that which parents often recognize as important, even without these formal frameworks. This information aims to inform and inspire, and one or more items may resonate with you.

"Habits and Mindsets" Frameworks	
Collaborative for Academic, Social and Emotional Learning (CASEL)	Social and emotional learning (SEL) is the process through which children and adults acquire and effectively apply the knowledge, attitudes and skills necessary to understand and manage emotions, set and achieve positive goals, feel and show empathy for others, establish and maintain positive relationships, and make responsible decisions. The five key competencies that CASEL has identified are self-awareness, self-management, social awareness, relationship skills and responsible decision-making.[25]

Think. Know. Act. Go. Educational Policy and Improvement Center (EPIC)	David Conley, a professor at the University of Oregon, defines college and career readiness as the "content knowledge, skills and habits that students must possess to be successful in postsecondary education or training that leads to a sustaining career." Conley describes four keys to college and career readiness for students: think deeply about what they are doing; know contextually when they learn; act purposefully to achieve their goals; and go successfully through life's transitions.[26]
Deeper Learning; The Hewlett Foundation	Deeper Learning is defined by six competencies: mastery of core academic content; critical thinking and problem solving; collaboration; effective communication; self-directed learning; and an academic mindset.[27]
Habits of Success; Summit Public Schools	Summit Public Schools, a network of charter secondary schools based in Redwood City, California, cultivates "Habits of Success" that empower students with the skills to become self-directed learners and lead to academic and personal success. The "Habits of Success" include: managing stress, persevering through a challenge, working well with others, setting goals and making plans.[28]

Growth Mindset	Developed by Stanford University Professor Carol Dweck, a growth mindset is the belief that abilities and intelligence develop through effort. This is in contrast to a fixed mindset, which is the belief that abilities can't change. Students who learn this mindset show greater motivation in school, better grades and higher test scores.[29]
Partnership for 21st Century Learning	The Partnership for 21st Century Learning believes in the importance of teaching students in ways that are relevant, hands-on and lead to success beyond school. They describe the 4 C's of 21st century learning as critical thinking, communication, collaboration and creativity.
Noncognitive Variables	William Sedlacek, a researcher and counselor at the University of Maryland, studied The Gates Millennium Scholars Program to learn what attributes proved predictors of college degree attainment for students of color. He found eight attributes that were higher predictors of success in college than either GPA or SAT/ACT scores: positive self-concept, realistic self-appraisal, skills at navigating systems and understanding and dealing with discrimination, preference for long-range goals over short-term or immediate needs, availability of a strong support person, successful leadership experience, demonstrated community service involvement and knowledge acquired in or about a field.[30]

Every Learner is Unique

As the discussion around mindsets and habits confirms, there's more to learning than academics. Even parents of very young children quickly learn that there are no "universal truths." No "formula" exists that works every time and for every child. (If you've ever tried to get an infant to sleep through the night, you understand this on a soul level.) But the simple realization that every child is in fact different deserves acknowledgement and attention in a manner often obscured by its frequent status as a mere "cliché."

For example, Carri had to learn that her oldest child needs food before her feet hit the floor each morning. (Who knew that a simple bowl of raspberries could turn a string of early morning battles into a tear-free wake-up with a happy child?) And Bonnie realized that her daughter needs lots of assurance before trying anything risky. ("Yes, you can walk on the balance beam by yourself.") When she was younger, one of Tom's daughters went with the flow; the other wanted to take charge. Parents only need to learn that every child is unique, and it takes time and attention to figure out each individual as a person and learner. Discovering each kid's true nature—his or her strengths, challenges, idiosyncrasies, dreams, fears—that's all we really need to know to be good parents. When parents figure out what works for their own kids, they're empowered in new and meaningful ways.

Children's intrinsic needs and interests drive early learning. Children learn instinctively. They learn to roll over, then sit, crawl and finally walk, often within the span of the first two years of life. They discover how to form sounds, then words and then sentences. "Children are born learning, and their brains develop at an enormous rate in the first few years of life," says Kris Perry of the First Five Years Fund, adding, "This is the time when they learn and develop the early cognitive and social skills that set the foundation for later success in school, career and life."

inspirational

Nurturing Passion and Authenticity

In <u>Why I Hate Pink: Abandoning Gender Stereotypes</u>, Caroline Vander Ark describes her feelings when she found out she was having a daughter. She explains, "The night I found out we were having a baby girl, I found myself wide awake in the middle of the night, panicked. Not because I wasn't excited for a girl, but because I feared she wouldn't grow up knowing she can be and do anything that she wants."

Reflecting on her own education and career gave her insights into her own parenting. She explains, "Our job as parents is to give children all the tools needed to figure out what they were meant to be. We should ignite passions, teach children to always be learning and help them see the world of choices available. Kids crave being around people that nurture their passions and help them learn who they are. By modeling the way in our house, splitting the household chores and both contributing equally to family discussions, my husband and I hope to provide a family life that encourages creativity and options. It may not seem like a bright-pink onesie with a silly saying is that serious, but to me, choices we make as parents before our children are even born will shape who they become and what they will think of themselves. So yes, our daughter may end up wearing pink, but she'll know that blue, orange, yellow and green are options, too. She'll know her parents support her and want her to always learn and grow as well as be respectful toward everyone she meets."[31] For more on issues related to gender and learning, see <u>Lessons For Parents on Pink Versus Blue Tech</u> from Dr. Alison Bryant.

Interests, driven by innate curiosities and needs, continue to be a powerful motivator for learning throughout childhood into adulthood, but they are seldom a priority of the formal education system. The goal of interest-driven learning ("for me") is satisfaction; it happens anywhere, anytime. Formal education ("for degree") has historically been sequential, structured, scheduled and school-based. Parents have the unique opportunity to encourage interest-based learning and to advocate for more of it at school.[32]

A parent's first job should be establishing the link between love and learning. In his best-seller, "A Road Less Traveled," M. Scott Peck defines love as extending yourself to serve another person's growth—a perfect description of a parent. The role of parent as Chief Growth Officer starts with making learning a priority and providing unconditional support, but that may not involve what you think. As we will further illustrate through all of the parent stories in this book, support does not mean doing the hard work for our kids. If only it were that easy. (Any parent who has attempted leaving the house with a child wanting to tie his or her own shoe knows how frustrating it can be to let your children do things for themselves.) Yet, encouraging your children to learn in ways that work well for them—and at their own pace—proves empowering and will serve them well as they get older. It's key to adjust the balance of expectations and support as the learner matures and becomes more independent.

Adaptive Learning

One of the most exciting developments in educational technology is adaptive learning—a game or activity that automatically responds to the individual student. For example, <u>DreamBox Learning</u>, an adaptive math program that moves learners through a series of mathematical skills in grades K-8, automatically adjusts the difficulty of each challenge based on how the learner performs during each task. When Carri's daughter tried DreamBox as a summer learning activity, she was immediately surprised by the challenges that the program kept throwing at her. After all, she'd always excelled at math in school, a subject that "came easily" for her. While getting summer math practice was an important result of using DreamBox, the most significant lesson for the soon-to-be second-grader went beyond that.

Carri and her daughter spent a lot of time talking about the learning process and the importance of challenges that sometimes arise. Carri told stories of her own struggles as a doctoral student and shared a hardbound copy of her dissertation as evidence of her hard work. Her daughter gained a better understanding and new sense of purpose—not only in the adaptive learning program, but in her regular classroom as well. In fact, teachers even noted this shift in the first parent-teacher conference of the year.

As anyone who has had to learn a new language or master trigonometry can attest, learning new things can be fun but also challenging. Bonnie's high school students used to complain that their brains actually "hurt" after practicing dialogues in Spanish and learning how to solve an algebraic equation. Although learning sometimes does "hurt," students often told Bonnie they felt empowered when they realized they could learn "hard" things and do complex work. Often, Bonnie noticed that the real power in learning came when students had choice over what and how they learned. When students create personalized plans with some choice over curriculum, pacing and location of learning, students own their own learning; they make action-oriented choices about their future and learn critical academic and personal skills that help them in college, career and beyond. Personalized learning plans will be discussed in further detail in Chapter Two, and more on learning plan design and templates to use at home can be found in the <u>Smart Parent Toolkit</u>.

Modeling the Way

Parents can model the reality that, although learning isn't always "easy," it can be a very powerful experience. In their evening discussions of the day's highlights and challenges, Carri encourages her daughters to describe something new they learned, something that challenged them or something they found frustrating. At first, her young kids struggled to find the language to explain their experiences in this way. Modeling this practice for them really helped. Both she and her husband now share pieces of their day and describe what they learned from each experience. They were surprised to learn that their own kids assumed that mom and dad moved through the world without obstacles or annoyances. Both girls were relieved to learn that struggles can be an opportunity to learn and grow—not something to be ashamed of or hide from.

Parenting for powerful learning involves having the tools and strategies so that parents can empower their children to learn in ways that are student-centered—meaning the learning has been crafted with the student and for the student.

As Nicholas Donohue writes in the introduction, the Nellie Mae Education Foundation offers a framework for student-centered learning opportunities, and the next four chapters explore student-centered learning as parenting principles for powerful learning. These principles will help you to guide your children: planning their path, finding their way, learning at their pace, and determining their place.

School Spotlights

We want our children to graduate from high school and earn their diplomas, but how do we know what those diplomas actually mean? (The "A" in Algebra II or the "B" in Chemistry might indicate different things at different schools.) When a child receives his or her diploma, what set of experiences does that represent? What has he or she really done or earned? And, what might the practical application of student-centered learning look like throughout your child's schooling?

One rural school district receiving national attention, Danville Schools, south of Lexington, Kentucky, describes what comes with a Danville diploma. Experiences include those that equip students with skills to persevere through potential challenges and that develop critical thinking skills. Students must demonstrate readiness to move to the next level at specific transition points (grades 5, 8 and 11) by showing growth and development as learners and ways they are a productive, contributing members of the school and larger community. The school board also requires meaningful, in-depth experiences for students in the areas of service learning and career interests, as well as ongoing opportunities to explore the visual and performing arts. Each year, starting no later than fifth grade, these opportunities allow students to plan ahead for college and future careers, with the purpose of exposing them to as many options as possible.

Additional meaningful experiences include the opportunity for students, beginning in kindergarten, to become conversant in one language other than English (or their native language), with the chance to explore linguistic learning through projects, exposure to financial literacy, an understanding of social media responsibility and development of responsible citizenship. School boards and leaders working to cultivate these types of experiences help to engage students' interests—creating opportunities for students to be at the center of their own learning.

As Mira Browne and Betty Chen of Summit Public Schools write in Graduating Self-Directed Learners Ready to Thrive in College, "Empowering our students with the skills to become self-directed learners will help them to develop the 'Habits of Success' that lead to academic and personal success. 'Habits of Success' are mindsets and behaviors such as managing stress, persevering through a challenge, working well with others, setting goals and making plans, all of which ultimately deepen life satisfaction. Similar to reading or writing, these skills can be learned through persistent practice and having strong role models. At Summit, our teachers dedicate at least 200 hours during the school year to mentoring and coaching students in their 'Habits of Success' through one-on-one mentor check-ins and other such practices. We nurture a community of learners in which our students can practice, model and reflect on these skills, plus they receive rich feedback from teachers and peers, helping them to individually grow and thrive."[33]

Parent Perspectives

The pages that follow feature these parent stories:

In <u>Growth Mindset Parenting</u>, Eduardo Briceño describes the powerful ways parents can support their children in the development of mindsets that activate lifelong learning.

In <u>Smart Parent Tip: See "Inside Out"</u>, Carri Schneider offers a review of the Pixar movie "Inside Out" and explains how the movie has helped her family in discussing the power of emotions.

In <u>Parenting for Social and Emotional Learning</u>, Jennifer Miller describes the importance of cultivating social and emotional growth in children, and she describes interactions with her son demonstrating the importance of those skills.

Growth Mindset Parenting
Eduardo Briceño

"Many of us want our children to understand that we love them and to believe that life can be fulfilling. Developing such beliefs will help them prosper. Another powerful, research-based belief exists that will also help children thrive; it's called a growth mindset.

What is a growth mindset? A growth mindset is the belief that we can develop our abilities, including our intelligence. A growth mindset is distinguished from a fixed mindset, which mandates that abilities can't change, for example, thinking that some people can't improve in math, creativity, writing, relationship-building, leadership, sports and so on.

The mindset that we adopt leads to very different behaviors, improvements and achievements. As an example, research conducted with adults shows that those who believe that good negotiators are made rather than born—a growth mindset about negotiation skills—tend to persevere in tough negotiations, create more collective value and capture more of the value in negotiations, as compared to those with a fixed mindset. Similarly, people who believe that leadership skills are developed— a growth mindset about leadership skills—feel inspired rather than threatened by other leaders, have higher confidence in their own ability to lead and experience lower anxiety and higher performance in leadership activities. Managers who believe that personal qualities can change are more likely to seek and welcome feedback, accurately notice changes in employee performance and take on more coaching-oriented behaviors, leading to improved team capability and performance. Additionally, lots of research shows that children with a growth mindset seek more effective learning strategies, work harder, persevere in the face of setbacks and achieve higher competence.

Why does this happen? It turns out that a fixed mindset, which views abilities as set, leads people to see effort as a sign of inability; this makes them feel badly about themselves when they need to expend effort, so they avoid it. But those with a growth mindset see effort as something that makes us smart and capable, so they seek it out. Second, people with a fixed mindset are mostly concerned with being seen as smart and talented by others, so they gravitate toward doing things they already know how to do quickly and perfectly. But those with a growth mindset can get bored when doing something they've already mastered, instead preferring to challenge themselves by learning something new, which is necessary for growth and improvement. And when they encounter setbacks or failures, people with a fixed mindset tend to conclude they're incapable, so to protect their ego, they lose interest and withdraw; on the other hand, those with a growth mindset understand that learning something new involves struggles and mistakes, so they persevere.

How can we develop a growth mindset in our children? Children learn whether abilities are fixed or malleable through their observations of the world. If we adults maintain a fixed mindset, we will behave and communicate in relevant ways—such as shying away from challenges or talking about people as if their abilities are fixed. This will tend to encourage a fixed mindset in our children, too. For example, when we believe that people are either smart or not, we may find ourselves praising our children for being smart, rather than acknowledging the effort or strategies that led them to success. We do that with only the best intentions, wanting to boost our children's confidence and self-esteem. But research shows that when we praise children for being smart, they adopt a fixed mindset (i.e., thinking that people are either smart or not); as a result, when things get hard for them, they conclude that they are not smart, and they experience higher anxiety, decreased confidence and lower performance. They also become less interested in learning and more interested in showing what they already know how to do. While being told they're smart may make them feel good in the short term, the deeper lesson indicates that people are either smart or not; consequently, when things get hard, they feel incapable."[34]

Smart Parent Tip: See "Inside Out"
Carri Schneider

"First swim meet of the season. Quite realistically one of the <u>largest pools in the country</u>. When the kids showed up for their warm-ups in the water, about half of the kids under 10 (including our Josephine) collapsed into tears. Fifty meters long. Nine feet deep. Fear. Panic. And from Josie, a string of sniffling: 'Mama please no. I can't. I know I can't.' In moments like this, everything you think you know about being someone's mother bubbles to the surface and explodes into thin air, leaving nothing but similar fear and panic. I knew she needed to just do it. I knew that I needed to tell her to just do it. I knew that through tears and pleading that she really did have it in her. Another parent I trust knew what I needed to hear at that moment, too. And so with an 'I love you,' a 'Honey, you've got this,' and a 'It's hard to understand right now, but this is a choice you get to make about how you want to live your life,' I adjusted her goggles, kissed her swim cap and hoped I had done the right thing. Tonight she overcame fears and found out what she was made of. She jumped into nine feet of water in a pool twice the length that she's used to and swam 50 meters of her most challenging stroke. She came away with a third-place and two first-place finishes. She struggled. She succeeded. And tonight at 11 p.m. when she was finally getting to bed, she told us about how she could hear the crowd cheering for her. And just before she closed her eyes, she thanked me.

I first shared this story <u>on Instagram </u>a couple weeks ago. That was before we saw the Disney Pixar movie 'Inside

Out.' While I wouldn't go back and change much about that life-defining moment for both my daughter and for me that night at the pool, it sure would've been convenient if I had the lessons from 'Inside Out' in my parenting toolbelt that night. I would've used the language we learned in the movie and, instead of letting fear 'drive' either of us in that moment, we would've taken a breath, acknowledged what was happening up in 'headquarters,' and gone to bed that night talking about the new 'core memory' that we formed together.

So what makes this film so special? Maybe it's the fruits of Pixar's landmark process that provides such inspiration and creativity. Maybe it's because 'Inside Out' is one of the most educational—and simultaneously entertaining—films ever to hit the big screen. Maybe it's the star power of the cast. Or, just maybe, this film has become such a hit because it resonates with parents and a growing movement that increasingly acknowledges the importance of social and emotional wellness, especially as it connects to learning. Really, it all comes down to a new way of thinking about social and emotional health—or just thinking about and acknowledging our emotions in general."[35]

The Power of Parenting with Social and Emotional Learning
Jennifer Miller

"On the 100th day of school, my son's teacher morphed each first-grade child's photograph into an elderly individual with the facial lines of life experience and asked, 'What do you want to be like when you are 100?' My son wrote in response, 'I want to be kind to kids.' And I immediately thought, 'Yes, me too.' It seems simple. But is it? As parents, we want to prepare our kids for success in life, but figuring out what that means and what steps can be taken toward that intention each day seems anything but simple. Yet these are undoubtedly questions worth asking. A recent survey from NBC's Parent Toolkit using the Princeton Survey Research Associates International found that the majority of U.S. parents interviewed ranked social and communication skills as most important for building success in school and life, even more than academic grades.

Social and emotional learning (SEL) involves acquiring and effectively applying knowledge, attitudes and skills to understand and manage emotions, set and achieve positive goals, feel and show empathy for others, establish and maintain positive relationships and make responsible decisions.

Fortunately, we don't have to make the choice between teaching social and emotional skills versus academic performance. In fact, one relies on the other, just like the head needs the heart. Essential life skills serve as a foundation for academic achievement, whether we define it by grade point averages, results from high-stakes tests or other measures of performance. And many schools not only make that connection, but they also implement research-based curricula that teach social and emotional learning alongside academic content.

While teaching skills like empathy, active listening and collaborative problem solving, schools can simultaneously prevent unhealthy, high-risk behaviors, including school violence. The <u>Collaborative for Academic, Social and Emotional Learning</u> (CASEL) examined more than 200 studies of schools with and without SEL programming and found an 11 percentile point advantage on achievement tests among students at schools that place an emphasis on both the head and heart. And this stands to reason; students well-practiced in problem solving and responsible decision-making will be better equipped to approach test questions with critical thinking skills.

Parents naturally worry about grade point averages, test scores and classroom performance. However, it turns out, numerous studies confirm that the foundation of relational trust between a student and teacher or among peers allows for deep learning to occur. Learning requires risk—often giant leaps of faith on the part of a student confronting failure over and over again—before mastery becomes possible. The student must trust that, even when feeling temporarily blinded by new concepts, the classroom is a safe place to take those risks, and the teacher will lead students along a path to clarity and understanding.

The close sense of attachment fundamental to parent-child relationships also forms in teacher-student bonds.

These connections occur throughout childhood and adolescence, not solely during the early childhood years, when it may appear more pronounced as children openly express their attachment through hugs and adoration. Since safety, trust and caring are all fundamental precursors for learning to establish meaningful connections with all caregivers, parents and teachers prove a necessary ingredient for student success."[36]

Key Points

 BE INFORMED. Technology is changing how we parent and how we learn, and parents now navigate an unprecedented number of educational options.

 BE INVOLVED. Student-centered learning represents an approach that will allow for greater degrees of engagement and personalization, marrying technology with a student-centered approach to the what, why, how, where and when children learn.

 BE INTENTIONAL. Cultivate social and emotional learning plus mindsets and habits that support lifelong learners.

 BE INSPIRATIONAL. Universal truths about parenting exist: Every child is unique, parents and mindsets matter, and the right types of support and advocacy prove critical for growth, development and lifelong learning.

In the Toolkit

Find specific ideas on how schools can encourage a growth mindset and how you can encourage growth mindsets at home.

Learn more about social and emotional learning, including specific strategies for parenting with social and emotional growth.

Gather additional resources on school choices and options.

Chapter 2:
Their Plan

What Personalized Learning Means in My Family
Marie Bjerede

"Our kids have been in Montessori, public school, private school, free and democratic school, home-schooled and unschooled according to what they needed most at any given time. What would a school look like that prepared my children for meaningful, authentic work and meaningful relationships? School would respect the natural rhythms of learning—periods of intense immersion and periods of collaborative exploration and periods of original creation and contribution. School would include experiences where my kids genuinely struggle—with systems thinking, with ethical thinking, with problem-solving, with collaborative work, with designing and doing, with experimentation and iteration—all within the context of real work, the kind where the experience of 'flow' is not only possible, but likely. School would engage my kids' unique strengths and talents and give them the experience of success as well as an appreciation of failure."[37]

Creating a Path of Personalized Learning

Personalized learning recognizes that students engage in learning in a variety of ways and according to their own unique needs. A personalized education experience:

- recognizes each child is unique.

- recognizes that each child learns in unique ways.

- allows the student to control some aspects of pacing to best learn (see more on "moving at one's own pace" in Chapter Three).

- addresses a child's current skill set and includes a plan for helping address his or her vision for personalized goals, both academic and personal.

- allows the student to develop and pursue interests.

- creates opportunities for assessment of skills in an ongoing manner that involves the student.

- values relationships with parents, teachers, mentors, tutors and coaches.

What does a personalized learning environment look like at home, at school or in other learning environments? Personalized learning means that students become actively involved in designing their own process and take responsibility for how they learn. They also have authentic choices about what they learn.

In the last several years, we have talked to hundreds of parents about school choices. Many parents with multiple children remark that they have been amazed and surprised by how individual children have different educational experiences—even if they have the same two parents! A high degree of personalization, through the creation of a learning plan and cultivation of individual needs, proves key in making student-centered choices about each child's educational journey.

In schools that support student-centered learning, students identify goals with guidance from a teacher, an advisor, mentor, tutor or counselor. Because of ubiquitous access to tools at home and at school, students can utilize technology to enhance learning and move at their own pace. The teacher/advisor, along with (in the best-case scenario) a learning plan team, support personalization by holding a student accountable to his or her own vision, goals and progress. The team of invested adults typically consists of parents, mentors, teachers, counselors and fellow students who help guide and support learning, placing the student at the center.

What's a Learning Plan?

A learning plan addresses important academic, college, career and personal competencies. It also contains a list of tasks to be accomplished and a plan for documenting and demonstrating learning. Typical components of personal learning plans include:

- a vision statement authored by the student, i.e., "What's your vision?"

- a goals list

- specific project lists

- tasks, deadlines and due dates, based on student goals and defined projects

---

- specific courses and career path options, depending on a student's age or grade level and based on each student's post-high school goals

Create a learning plan. Ask your son or daughter:

- "What do you want to know more about?"

- "How can you get there?"

- "How will you know you've learned this piece of information?"

Who's on a learning plan team? A learning plan team can consist of anyone who supports and encourages student learning. This can be (but is not limited to) parents, teachers, counselors, tutors, coaches, mentors, other family members and student peers.

How often do learning plan teams meet? Members of the learning plan team should all meet formally every three months with weekly, informal check-ins with a teacher or advisor. Meetings involve touching base with the student to ask about his or her work and progress, holding students accountable to achieving pre-established goals and setting new ones. Meetings also help maintain progress toward standards-aligned curriculum and ensure Deeper Learning to facilitate college and career preparation.

See the Learning Plan Template in the Smart Parent Toolkit.

Here are some questions and conversations you can have at home to help your students build, drive and own their learning.

Age	Purpose	Learning Plan Tips
Early Childhood Learners	Talking to—and getting to know—your unique child is critical at this early age. The brain develops so rapidly, and children have a natural and innate curiosity that parents can activate. See Early Childhood Education is Critical for Your Own Kids' Future—and the Nation's.	Encourage your child to ask you questions.
Elementary School Learners	Setting the stage during early school years activates a love of learning and starts healthy habits of the mind and positive learning strategies for years to come. See 10 Ways to Inspire A Love of Learning.	Share your own experiences and model your own curiosities out loud.
Middle School Learners	It's never too early to think about the future. As middle school students develop their own identities, it's important to ensure they can see the "bigger picture," pursue their unique interests, and contemplate their contributions. See Understanding Your Middle Schooler: 4 Tips for Success.	Allow your middle schooler to explore his likes or dislikes in the context of shifting identities and friendships.
High School Learners	The future is imminent, and so much needs to be done in the high school years to prepare for college, careers and lifelong learning. The teenage brain is ripe for further discovery, and teens seek to learn their place in the world. Although they sometimes might not seem like it, teens do still want and need their parents. See The Teenage Brain: Scaffolding the Brain for Lifelong Learning.	Offer support and guidance.

Components of Personalized Learning

Personalized learning allows students to describe a plan for academic and personal growth based on where they are, where they want to be, and where they need to be. This then becomes the curriculum and blueprint for a student's learning journey. Adults who have strong relationships with their students can play a significant role in helping guide and support a student's learning path. Those same adults also provide feedback on a student's progress and help hold students accountable to meeting academic and personal goals described within the plan.

A personal learning plan can look different depending on the school or learning environment—and, of course, the student. Schools will often evaluate and assess students based on goals that have been created in concert with parents, teachers and advisors. Goals crafted with educators can be aligned to high standards and Deeper Learning outcomes that are associated with a higher degree of student engagement and success in college and careers.

Personalized learning helps students in three specific ways. First, teaching students to set short- and long-term goals and to track their own academic and personal growth in and outside of the classroom increases student motivation and engagement. Second, empowering students to explore areas of interest and build sustained relationships with adults creates new learning opportunities. Finally, by encouraging the writing of vision statements and goals, particularly in middle and high school years, we broaden the exposure of all students to college and career options, thus preparing high school students for the task of directing their own lives by providing sustained support for post-high school planning.[38] All children need high expectations, and all children deserve high levels of support.

Eight Secrets of Powerful Learning

Kathleen Cushman, author of the book "What Kids Can Do," interviewed kids about motivation, learning and mastery. It turns out, kids have a lot of advice to offer adults about how they best learn. Cushman calls these the "eight universal secrets of powerful, personalized learning:

1. **We feel OK.** Creating well-being in a learning environment is the crucial first step, according to both kids and scientists. Threats to our physical or emotional safety—from hunger to humiliation— shut down learning as we respond to more primal signals.

2. **It matters.** A personal connection or a real-world issue can make all the difference to whether we care about an academic task. Offering a choice on some aspect of the project also increases its value, as does the chance to work on things with friends.

3. **It's active.** From constructing a model to collaborating on a puzzle, we start to 'own' new information when our hands and minds engage our thinking processes more fully.

4. **It stretches us.** Extreme frustration can shut down learning, but a stretch that's both challenging and achievable gives the learner a buzz of excitement. (Don't forget to notice small successes along the way!)

5. **We have a coach.** We do much better with someone around who will help us make sure we're getting it right—watching us practice and providing tips,

while giving plenty of time to learn from our mistakes.

6. **We have to use it.** Doing something with information not only shows that we know it, but also makes the knowledge stick in our minds. The most fun option involves performing what we've learned or teaching it to others, but even a pop quiz will do the trick.

7. **We think back on it.** What did I learn? What would I do differently next time? How have I grown and changed? Making time for us to reflect on questions like these has a huge effect on deepening our learning, yet it's the easiest thing to skip.

8. **We plan our next steps.** Planning any venture— an argument, a project, even what we're going to say next—is a creative adventure. It forces us to remember information in order to develop an idea or solve a problem. Hand us the keys to our learning, and watch us take those intellectual risks!"[39]

We should keep Cushman's eight universal truths in mind as we interact with our children and encourage them to activate their own interests and pursue their education in a personalized way. When families, students and educators work together and holistically approach children's education, focusing on children's academic, social and emotional needs, we sow the seeds for powerful learning.

In evaluating learning materials and environments for our children, it's also helpful to keep the eight universal truths in mind. These empower students, encourage exploration, instill passion and inspire a love of learning. When we stay committed to a philosophy of student-centered learning, we listen to our children, allow them to make mistakes, ask them lots of questions, encourage them to reflect, and model the way.

Demonstrations of Learning

Students should demonstrate their learning to parents, teachers and public audiences on a regular basis—several times each year at a minimum. Typically, culminating extended projects and demonstrations in front of an audience can be a powerful experience. Bonnie worked at a high school where every student led an exhibition of his or her work at least three times per year. The exhibitions often proved an excellent example of personalization and were often a "game changer" for students. At their best, exhibitions became a powerful example of highly-personalized, authentic and student-led learning.

When given the opportunity to spend six months visiting the best schools in the country, Tom discovered that good schools engage their students in relevant challenging projects and ask them to make regular demonstrations of learning. While leading education at the Bill & Melinda Gates Foundation, he had the opportunity to sponsor 1,200 new schools that incorporated these powerful strategies. More recently, Tom and Carri profiled 20 of these schools in a paper, Deeper Learning for Every Student Every Day, demonstrating that these strategies can be used by any school to engage, inspire and prepare students.

Public demonstrations of learning provide students an opportunity to learn how to speak in front of others. Of course, this can cause some anxiety for students, so the first few times a student does this, they need to be given ample time to practice, receive feedback on their warm-up sessions, and haven opportunities to watch other students in action. The audiences include parents, teachers, mentors and guests from the local school district or community, and student peers, who often hold high expectations for their fellow students. Highly-personalized evaluations of student goals and progress—both personally and academically—result when the student presents by him or herself in this manner.

In their personalized learning plans, students are able to articulate how they will demonstrate their knowledge and assessment through more than tests. In personalized learning environments, schools encourage digital portfolios of student work. A collection of personal bests can be stored in the cloud and viewed anywhere on any device. Learners can receive (and act on) feedback from teachers or their parents, mentors, teachers or peers in real time. (For more on anytime and anywhere learning, see Chapter Four.) Imagine that a student began tracking his or her college readiness work in the 7th grade and continued to do so through the 12th grade. In addition to providing examples of quality work, portfolios can contain student resumes, essays for colleges and scholarships, research related to colleges and majors, college testing preparation, career explorations and post-high school vision statements. (See Personalizing and Guiding College and Career Readiness for more on portfolios.)

In addition to including specific academic work in their personal learning plan, students may include growth and development related to learning skills and habits of mind we discussed in the first chapter. Bonnie has seen examples of personal learning plans that include students' desires to work on their time management skills, their physical and personal fitness and even their health. Bonnie remembers a student whose learning plan had detailed goals around wellness and student projects that included meditation, healthy eating and learning to cook vegan meals.

This holistic approach to learning echoes the experience of Carri's children in their Montessori classrooms—a model of learning often described as one of the earliest foundations for personalized, student-centered learning. In a Montessori classroom, students spend time daily moving through their own "work cycle" across content like mathematics and language but also "practical life" skills such as washing, sewing and preparing food.

Demonstrations of learning can be a great summer, family-based learning activity. Tom helped his daughters shape annual summer learning projects often connected to a family trip, i.e., French Impressionist art during a visit to Paris. The investigation allowed the children to become tour guides for portions of the trip. Projects culminated in a report and a PowerPoint presentation delivered to friends and family.

The performing arts offer opportunities for wonderful, often life-changing, demonstrations of learning. After attending the National Choral Directors Conference where her son performed, our colleague Mary Ryerse reminded us, "Music fosters cross-curricular learning and builds an innovation mindset—combining effort, initiative and collaboration." She noted an interesting similarity to the maker movement in which young people see the rewards of initiative in tangible ways.[40]

Personal learning plans may even include outside learning opportunities such as internships or community service. The 667 National Academy Foundation academies ask students to demonstrate learning through a combination of coursework and internships where employers provide feedback on seven dimensions. In Houston, Texas, students at Quest Early College High School plan for about 400 hours of service that often includes an internship. Service

Learning Coordinator Jim Nerad ensures a high level of student preparation. The articulate upper division students we spoke with said their service learning experience helped them mature and gain confidence in work settings.[41]

A personal learning plan that contains goals related to academics and personal growth empowers parents and mentors to serve as learning advocates.

Parent Advocacy

As mother Nancy Weinstein declares, parents are the "Chief Advocates." In Parents as Chief Advocates, Nancy writes: "Did you know that, in addition to your responsibilities of Chief Caregiver, Chief Cheerleader and Chief Taxi driver, Chief Advocate is high on the list? If you have a child with special needs, you know exactly where I'm going with this. For those who aren't familiar, you should know that at some point, your child, every child, will need help in a specific class, with a teacher who is not meeting their needs, with a previously undetected learning problem, with bullying. It's the problem that doesn't go away in a week, or even a month. It impacts self-esteem and starts to look like depression or anxiety. And you, my fellow parent, are the only one who will understand the depth of the problem. You will be the one to see the nightly struggle with homework, the tears that wait for the comfort of home, the lack of appetite, the lack of sleep. And then your time as Chief Advocate has arrived."[42]

Consider the story of parent Karen Copeland, who writes the blog Champions for Community Mental Wellness. She realized when her son started kindergarten that school was going to look much different for him than it did for his sister. In I am "That" Parent, Karen writes, "I started out not really knowing how to advocate for my son and his learning needs, but I persisted. I took the time to figure out how my son learns, eventually discovering his strengths and gifts. Even though my son learns differently, this is not something to be ashamed of; it is something to celebrate because it challenges me to think in new—and often better—ways ... We have figured out that creating positive connections with supportive adults has made an incredible difference in our son's confidence. Those trusting relationships have given my son the chance to discover that other adults believe in him, too. That he is good enough ... I am proud of myself for becoming more knowledgeable about the challenges my child faces, learning about the systems we access for support, learning the jargon so I don't feel dumb sitting at the meeting table when an acronym is used ... I am glad to have discovered my voice—that I have become aware of my rights as a parent in these systems, and I am not afraid to let this be known."[43]

We're Inspired By You:
The Smart Parents Blog Series

Throughout the course of our Smart Parents blog series, we have heard from many passionate parents about how they advocate for their students. The most inspiring blog articles in our series came from parents of students who have learning and/or physical disabilities and need additional and individualized support. As parents, when we read stories about the work that these parents have done to advocate for their students, we are both inspired and moved. This book and the accompanying Smart Parent Toolkit were written in large part out of a desire to share those stories.

Parents play a crucial role in in advocating for their children. Parent advocates also help ensure that others—including teachers, mentors, tutors, coaches and even siblings—become advocates as well. Parent advocacy will of course look different for each individual child.

Parent organizer Jose Arenas of <u>Innovate Public Schools</u> encourages parents in his article <u>Organized Parents Can Transform Public education – Indeed, It Won't Happen Without Them</u> to become involved in the public arena. While we all may not be on the school board or involved in ground-level local politics, Jose makes a strong case for parents' role in advocating for changes at the policy level: "Public institutions tend to be only as effective as the public demands they be. The people closest to a problem are often the ones best able to identify and realize the solution. A healthy democracy with effective public schools depends on having informed and engaged citizens who are connected to their community leaders and each other. Innovate Public Schools works with passionate parent leaders in Silicon Valley and the Bay Area who want to improve local schools and help them to connect to one another and to build their collective power to make real and lasting change in their community...More than two dozen parent leaders have driven the campaign to improve public education in Redwood City. Over two years, they engaged over 900 other parents in the community, met with more than 25 elected officials and community leaders and planned and ran two standing-room-only community action forums to ask elected officials to share their perspectives and pledge their public commitment to working with parents. Thanks to their efforts, two new schools are opening in Redwood City this fall and the district is implementing major efforts to turn around one of its persistently low-performing schools. These parents haven't called it a day. They're still organizing the community, making calls and going to school board and city meetings, and they won't stop until every child really is getting a great education. That's the power of organized parents."[44]

As mother and education policy expert Karla Phillips explains in her article <u>A Choosy Mom on Choosing Schools</u>, "Finding and choosing a good school is no easy task, especially if you have a child with special needs. Recent literature bears this out, and I can certainly testify to it. But I want my fellow parents in the trenches of IEP (individualized education plan) meetings to remember that our children are students first and a diagnosis second."[45]

<u>Trust Parents with Educational Choice</u>
Beth Purcell

"Put educational decisions in the hands of parents by giving us options and trust us to make the right choices to meet educational needs. Parents are trusted to pay taxes to support education, so why, then, aren't parents trusted to choose the right school for their children? For far too long, parents' voices have not been heard, and parents haven't been trusted to know what's best for their children. A parent knows a child's motivations, a child's fears, a child's strengths and a child's weaknesses.

I don't need state tests to tell me how a school is performing when I see my child being successful every day. I don't need a legislator or the state board of education to tell me whether or not a school is doing its job. Trust me to walk if my child's needs are not being met ... I have, and I will again, if I need to.

For 17 years, we have examined every decision we have made through the lens of how it will affect our two children. Like other parents, we have sacrificed much for our children, to make sure that they have the very best that we can give them—the best of everything and that includes education. There is no one in this world I trust more than me when it comes to my children. No one knows my children better than I do. No one will make better choices for them than I will. Trust parents."[46]

An Arizona Department of Education study found that schools with six key traits improved outcomes for all students. These traits are:

1. High Expectations

2. Highly-Effective Teaching Strategies

3. Data-Driven Decision-Making

4. Students Are Provided with Reteach and Enrichment Activities

5. Students with Disabilities Receive Core Instruction in the General Education Classroom

6. Effective Leadership[47]

Karla writes, "While it is important that our children are safe and provided the services and supports that they need to succeed, it is just as important that the school have the six qualities listed above because all of our kids deserve a great school."[48]

Advocacy means supporting a student's individual needs to be successful on his or her own. Lara Allen and her husband Curt Allen, CEO of <u>Agilix</u> and co-parent of the couple's five children, write: "When Lara goes to parent-teacher conferences she says: 'The first and last concern I have as a mother is whether or not our kids are learning and practicing compassion; yes, academic growth is critical, but trusting the teachers to teach and empower our kids to follow through and take on responsibility to demonstrate compassion and empathy is of greater concern. They learn best when they feel safe ... I will always help when they ask for it and will always require work before play, but I will never do the work for them.'"[49]

A critical parent role involves helping teachers gain insight into a child as a learner and sharing information about a student's home life. . Educators can make the conversation easier by opening multiple lines of communication. When Tom was a public school superintendent, the district opened an office in a mall to make it easier for parents to get school information and enroll their children. Tom spent weekends in the mall and visited faith congregations to meet parents on their terms and in a comfortable space.

When Bonnie started teaching, she visited the homes of many of her students as part of an initiative to encourage strong school and family partnerships. In doing so, she gained a deeper understanding of where her students came from, their family life and family history, and the values the students (and their parents) held dear. And because of these home visits, Bonnie developed a stronger partnership with many of her students' families. Parents also had access to Bonnie's phone number and email, and they could call if something was going on with their student. This was all to help Bonnie and other adults at the school offer better support. She and her principal once met a family at McDonald's—all part of the "we will meet you whenever and wherever" approach to supporting students and families.

When parents and educators collaborate, they can form a balanced picture of each child that ultimately benefits the child at home and at school.

Relationships Matter

Why Mentors Matter
Sarah Vander Schaaff

"During my senior year in high school, just about when the pressure of life and the ambivalence of graduation overwhelmed me, my dear drama teacher summoned me to his office from gym class. We both needed a break, he said. We hopped in his red and white pick-up truck and headed to the best bakery in Austin.

Mr. Preas was my mentor. He taught me the discipline and craft of acting and took my work seriously, even though I was a young performer. He believed in me and encouraged me to have faith in myself. One day, probably a few months after that muffin run, when a telegram arrived stating some good news about my place in a national arts competition, he burst into my typing class and read the note for all to hear. Our typing drill simply had to wait as he read the short sentences with Texas pride.

Mr. Preas smoked during rehearsal, swore at times and had little patience for the juvenile behavior of those he called 'yahoos.' But he was devoted to his job, and he was devoted to anyone who wanted to learn. He entered my life during the rocky but exciting time of adolescence and gave me a place to explore friendships, dramatic literature, the human condition and even heartache. He was exactly what a young person seeks in a mentor. Parents may provide unconditional love, but a mentor's encouragement means something else; it means the world outside your familial nest sees something in you."[50]

When Bonnie taught high school students, she had a student whose mother was in jail. Fortunately for this student, his dad played a big part in his life. His father visited the school frequently. He emailed Bonnie, texted her often and set up meetings to check on his son's progress. Not only did the student's dad play an active role in his son's life, but he also mentored others. The father owned his own construction company. This was a field that interested many students. This student's father agreed to be a mentor and offered high school internships at his construction business.

Non-parent relationships can play a significant role in a child's life and can help create and spark learning and interests. At a young age, these non-parental mentors may show up in the role of a teacher or a sports coach. As students get older, mentors may be teachers, religious leaders or others in the community. During the teen years, as students become increasingly mobile, they are able to interact with a wide swath of adults and learn from people in the larger community. Mentors can play a direct role in cultivating, evaluating and advocating for the creation of powerful learning experiences.

Why do these mentor relationships matter so much? And why, as a parent, should I even want my child to have a mentor?

When teaching at a small high school south of Seattle, Bonnie saw the everyday impact that mentors could have. Students who had mentors were more organized, had stronger intellectual habits, and possessed increased confidence and self-awareness. Many of her students had mentors to assist with projects related to student interests, and some were very involved in the daily education of her students. For example, one student was interested in learning more about the legal profession. In the 9th grade, he obtained an internship with a father-daughter law practice in our community. Initially, this student struggled in our school; he had arrived already behind in reading and math. Yet, his two mentors not only had him help with work at their law firm, but they also spent hours assisting him in honing his reading skills. By the time he was in the 12th grade, this student had become a highly-skilled reader and writer; he was so passionate about the field of law that he earned an internship with a mentor who was a trial court judge in King County (Washington state) Superior Court. Bonnie had other students with mentors who were equally active and involved in her students' lives.

Some examples include mentors:

- In the automotive, constructive and welding industries, where students had hands-on experiences in work-based learning.

- At corporate headquarters, including Starbucks, where students interned in accounting, marketing and communications offices.

- In schools, where students assisted teachers, nutrition services, para-educators, principals, office managers and more.

- At their own businesses, including those in such fields as fitness, cosmetology, real estate and employment recruiting.

A Mentoring Program That Works

Communities in Schools coordinates dozens of academic and non-academic supports that help students stay in school and succeed in life, with mentoring playing a key role. While meeting basic needs proves important, it's the accumulation of support services that turns students around, including a caring adult who models a productive life and career. Without a caring adult, all of those other important supports are compromised.[51]

With increased access to technology, virtual mentors have become a possibility. For example, a student of Bonnie's had always wanted to create anime art. She had been a member of the DeviantArt community for years, and she was able to incorporate this interest into her schoolwork, turning her passion into projects such as creating her own thriving online art business, where she was paid to draw anime characters. It's great that such students who have niche interests can connect with expert mentors to learn more about their interests. Programs like College Bound and Strive for College also offer virtual mentoring. Students can work with adults from a distance, communicating over email, Skype, Google Hangouts, Facebook and texting. Virtual mentoring shares the goal of face-to-face mentoring: to establish a nurturing and trusting relationship between the student and mentor. (We will talk more about increased access to learning anytime and anywhere in Chapter Four.)

School Spotlights

Schools that value personalized learning help their students create personalized learning plans and achieve positive outcomes for students. In 2014, the Stanford Center for Opportunity Policy in Education (SCOPE) conducted research at four schools, providing independent evidence that student-centered practices increase academic achievement.[52]

The schools in the study used either the model from Linked Learning Alliance or Envision Schools—both show clear evidence of developing high levels of proficiency for students of color, English learners and low-income students at levels that far exceed traditional schools serving similar students.

How are they doing it? The strategies include:

- A commitment to personalized learning: Teachers dedicate themselves to meeting the unique needs of each student and creating learning plans with students and a learning plan team.

- Positive student-teacher relationships: Teachers build strong connections with their students and stay with them throughout their four years of high school.

- Reflection and revision: Performance-based assessments are designed to give students opportunities to practice, improve and demonstrate their skills and knowledge.[53]

In Charge: Student-Led Conferences
tinyurl.com/VIDEO-In-Charge

At <u>Pittsfield Middle High School</u> in New Hampshire, students take the reign of traditional parent-teacher conferences. Students take the lead role in presentations that articulate academic, personal and social growth.

Parent Perspectives

The pages that follow feature these parent stories:

In <u>What Relationships Drive Learning? Try Fathers</u>, Patrick Riccards describes the role that dads play in encouraging powerful learning.

In <u>Ready for the World: Redefining Success in the Age of Change</u>, Antonia Slagle describes her son's journey through school fueled by a highly personalized experience at The Met School in Sacramento, California.

What Relationships Drive Learning? Try Fathers
Patrick Riccards

Last year, I learned of a school that was so excited to have a father come in and volunteer that it decided to throw a huge party in honor of the father. It's alarming that staff members deemed it so unique for a dad to volunteer at a school that they thought he should be celebrated, regaled and placed on a pedestal for taking out time from his busy life.

As mothers across the country grapple with the notion of "leaning in" and consistently hear how they need to be more like men—sacrificing family and personal needs for work, if they want to be truly professional—perhaps we need to flip that thinking. Maybe, just maybe, we should be talking about how dads should be more involved in their children's learning—how men need to look beyond the annual back-to-school nights or evening homework checks to actually roll up their sleeves and be active, positive, regular presences in their children's learning experience.

Don't get me wrong, I'm not saying engaged fathers don't exist. We all know dads who are highly involved in their local schools and in their kids' learning. But we should view that as the norm rather than the exception. We should come to expect it of all fathers, rather than make it seem special when it happens.

When my children first started school, I was a "work-comes-first" type of father. I justified that my primary duty was to earn a living and ensure that my kids were never wanting—providing a good home, a full fridge, a closet of clothes, even their own iPads. While my family remained the focus of my life, I attended to them by working harder and longer hours. I was the provider. Unfortunately though, that tablet proves an inadequate substitute for an involved parent. By spending more time in my kids' school, I realized the potential impact my presence could have, both on their learning and on their social development. I knew that my time was far more valuable than the latest electronic device.

Of course, this is not to say that dads should quit their jobs and commit their lives entirely to their children's educations. Nor is it implying that a father can't be active in the learning experience and still be professionally successful. It means that fathers need to work at it. We need to fight each day to find that balance. We need to look at how we can constantly improve to help our kids develop into the inquisitive, interesting, successful people that we all hope they will become.

With my son, it means using tablets as both a learning platform and a reward. In class, I noticed that he would hold a traditional book like it was a ticking bomb. Or he would look for ways to avoid needing to read, in part because he struggles as a reader. However, get him home, give him a tablet, and watch him go, thanks to the availability of an unlimited library and programs that will read with him along the way. We now leverage his love for Minecraft to develop his math skills; it is absolutely incredible what he can design with Minecraft. And it has extended to reading, as we discovered a Kindle novel collection set in the Minecraft world—books of which my struggling reader just can't get enough.

My children have grown up watching technology drive my life. As toddlers, they knew that if my cell phone rang or my smartphone indicated an incoming message, they should bring it to me immediately. They could model my behavior, knowing how to hold a device or make motions to have it perform as intended.

But the real power of technology comes from understanding what's being discussed in my kids' classes, seeing their strengths, and knowing how to supplement what's happening at school. The true benefits stem from seeing where they struggle and embracing where they soar. Such determinations can't be made from a report card, an email from the teacher or a quick review of the evening's homework. They require hands-on knowledge that comes from being in the classroom and witnessing the learning process.

In discussions about achievement gaps and struggling schools, the family dynamic usually gets a secondary mention, after poverty and finances. We know that fathers play an important role in their kids' lives. We cite the father dynamic regularly, whether through graduation tallies or crime rates.

So why do we pay so little attention to the role of the father in the learning experience? If the presence of a father in a child's life has such impact, think about all a dad can do when he's active in the schools and involved in the learning process.

Last year, a study in Psychological Science found that daughters aspire to greater professional goals when they see their fathers performing tasks such as washing the dishes. Consider that for a moment. A young girl has a better chance of become a CEO or governor or even president if she sees her dad at the sink, scrubbing away at the remnants of dinner.

If that's true, imagine the possibilities for all of those girls (and boys) who also see their dads volunteering at school or visiting the classroom, right alongside the moms whose presence they've come to expect. Envision how much more interesting that science project will look when dad comes into the class to help—or how intriguing the field trip might seem with dad leading a group. Also consider how that device can be transformed from a Netflix entertainment machine to a learning device that opens up new worlds and unlimited possibilities.[54]

Ready for The World: Redefining Success in the Age of Change
Antonia Slagle

At an early age, my son demonstrated the qualities of someone who was either going to rule the world or die trying. He questioned everything and everyone; quite frankly, it was a little bit exhausting. When Noah was younger and I was less knowledgeable, I was way more coercive in my style of parenting. I needed to contain him—or so I thought.

Fortunately, I entered the teaching field as he started kindergarten. Suddenly, I was not only immersed in educational theory, but also with real-life teenage subjects—all with their own personalities, needs and interests. And most of them questioned the relevance of what I was teaching them: How are they going to use this in "the real world"? Good question. I started to question my own views on what it means to be educated in a rapidly-changing world.

It didn't take long for me to figure out there had to be a better way to help my son navigate life, not just as a kid in my house, but as a citizen of the world. He needed more than reading, writing and arithmetic. He needed experience.

As Noah neared high-school age, we went looking for an educational experience to match his fierce independence and budding passions. We wanted an environment that wouldn't squash his spirit. Thankfully, during his 8th-grade year we discovered The Met Sacramento, a Big Picture Learning school. Our friend's son attended the school, and it sounded pretty incredible. Personalized, real-world learning? Internships, projects and dual enrollment opportunities? We were both sold.

My son and I started at The Met on the same day—he as a freshman, me as a teacher advisor. We never looked back.

While my son had to do certain things as a Met student, the manner in which Noah did them now became his own choice. My son co-wrote a learning plan every quarter with his advisor and created a portfolio of his work. He also presented his learning to a panel of peers and adults for feedback and support. He built websites, edited films and learned construction (among many other things) at his internships. Noah also had two key people at his side the whole time who got to know him and always challenged him: his mentor Steve and his advisor David.[55]

Key Points

 BE INFORMED. Personalized learning means allowing students to activate their interests and choose what they want to learn, aligned with high standards and college and career readiness.

 BE INVOLVED. Non-parent relationships are significant for students, and the role that coaches, mentors and teachers can play has an impact on personalization and academic success. Become a mentor to other students.

 BE INTENTIONAL. Model lifelong learning with your own children by sharing your own intellectual curiosities and learning goals.

 BE INSPIRATIONAL. You can create a learning plan at home and share it with your child's teacher.

In the Toolkit

Learn more about creating a <u>learning plan</u> at home.

See our <u>checklist</u> for how to determine if your child's school is student-centered.

Advocate for your students with <u>tips</u> from parents who have been there.

pace

Chapter 3:
Their Pace

Why Online Learning Works for My Family
Angela Shelton-Garofano

"One reason I opted for online school as opposed to traditional homeschool was the factor of lessons and lesson planning. I was a teacher for nine years, so I know how to plan lessons, but I was worried about finding the best lessons, staying on track and even what to plan. With online school, that's all taken care of for me. We have our weekly schedule that we can abide by as-is, or I can alter it for various reasons to fit what we have going on that week. Each Sunday I sit down and print us both a copy of the plan for the week and make notes on my son's, telling him workbook page numbers and whatnot. We like to do different subjects on the same day, so we keep the schedule as-is for the most part; but I like how I have the flexibility to change it and do math all one day and language arts another day if I choose to. I also appreciate the fact that, while attendance is tracked, it's not tracked on a daily basis. As long as progress is being made in the coursework, then all is well. If my son is having a bad day or if we have to attend to my daughter that day, then I can move our lessons around and not do school for the day. And since he's only doing necessary work and not 'busy work,' we finish much earlier than he used to at his old school, leaving us time for piano lessons, swimming and other various activities that we couldn't do before."[56]

Showing What They Know, Moving at Their Speed

Imagine a 5th-grade classroom where the teacher instructs students on how to divide fractions. Some students may understand the concepts, while others may be scratching their heads. Others may not even know how to divide whole numbers, making the concept of dividing fractions frustrating or downright impossible without a chance to learn prior competencies. A teacher with 25 to 30 students of varying abilities in any subject has his or her hands full. It's hard to imagine meeting all the students' needs in such an environment, and yet teachers are tasked with this job every day.

Choosing their own pace empowers students, leads to higher degrees of engagement and allows teachers to focus on students' strengths and deficits, rather than moving all students along at the same pace. Many traditional schools advance students to the next grade each year, regardless of whether they have mastered the knowledge and skills within a specific course or subject.

Age-based cohorts and grade-level matriculation (moving on to the next grade based on one's birthday rather than a demonstration of knowledge and skills) is one of the founding principles on which our American education system has been built. In high school, progress shifts from age to credit accumulation (toward a state-required minimum number of credits), but most credits reflect hours spent in a seat versus demonstrated mastery.

Students often enter high school with huge variations in terms of skills in the basics: reading, writing and math. For example, some students may have 5th-grade reading, writing or math skills because they have been socially promoted in order to stay with their grade level. Other students may be ahead in reading and math. In this scenario, a more advanced student may express profound boredom in his or her middle school experience. This could lead to disengagement from being the class "smart kid" and having to constantly review material that's already been mastered. Unfortunately, this example is not hypothetical. As educators, we've all seen how "teaching to the middle" can be harmful for students at every level by not adequately addressing everyone's needs.

Fortunately, leveraging advancements in technology allows students to move at their own pace. Personalized education options now utilize emerging educational technology so students can control their pace and path through content and materials. Students move on when they are ready, usually on demonstrating that they've mastered a specific skill, instead of moving on based on the school calendar or group lesson plan.

Moving at a student's own pace is also called competency-based (or proficiency- or mastery-based) learning. Nellie Mae Education Foundation explains that this type of system is "based primarily on mastery of a skill or body of knowledge, rather than age, hours on task or credits earned."[57] States have begun to adopt flexible measures so that students can graduate from high school according to competency-based mastery rather than through typical credit matriculation. Some states have even begun to change education policies so that students graduate from high school based on competency and mastery rather than through traditional credits and "seat-time." As technology becomes more ubiquitous, more options for students to learn at their own pace will continue to arise. Parents can support "at pace" learning by making school choices that take into account students' individual needs and by supporting and encouraging students to move at their own pace while learning outside of school. (The two parent stories at the end of this chapter demonstrate how this can be done effectively.)

There are three key benefits of competency-based learning:

- **First, it is personalized, not "one size fits all".**
  In a competency-based system, the student's individual needs and interests become the focus of all teaching efforts. Because it's personalized, it is harder for students to fall through the cracks; teachers and parents know how a student is doing and can ensure that he or she has the support needed to succeed.

- **Second, competency-based learning better prepares students.** By focusing on the mastery of critical knowledge and skills, competency-based pathways prevent learning gaps from developing and growing over time. As a result, this approach keeps students on the path to graduate from high school ready for college and careers.

- **Finally, competency-based learning is transparent.** Diplomas and transcripts from schools that use a competency-based model clearly communicate a student's level of preparation and give parents, college admissions counselors and employers a more complete sense of what a student has in fact learned.

Chris Sturgis, co-founder of CompetencyWorks, explains: "Student agency changes the nature of the educational process. As students build their habits of learning, they can take on more and more responsibility over their own education. The more experiences they have in managing their education, the more opportunities they have to strengthen their skills in time management, project management, pacing management and executing with professionalism."

In a competency-based education system:

- Students advance on mastery.

- Competencies include explicit, measurable, transferable learning objectives that empower students.

- Assessment goes beyond a single test score. It is ongoing, meaningful and diverse to inform progression through content.

- Students receive timely support, based on their individual learning needs.

- Learning outcomes emphasize competencies that include application and creation of knowledge, along with the development of important skills and dispositions.[58]

Advocacy for Competency-Based Learning

Competency Works, an advocate for competency-based education, cites three reasons for supporting it:

- To ensure that all students succeed in building college and career readiness, consistent with world-class knowledge and skills.

- To take advantage of the extraordinary technological advances in online learning for personalization, allowing students to learn at their own pace, anytime and anywhere. (See Chapter 8 for more on anytime, anywhere learning.)

- To provide greater flexibility for students who would otherwise not graduate from high school because they have to work or care for their families.[59]

The exponential growth of technology has aided in the advancement of competency-based learning. Blended and online learning options (further discussed in Chapter Four and defined in the glossary; see Appendix C) offer opportunities for students to self-pace and for teachers to guide based on where students land in terms of skills and academic readiness.

School Spotlights

Virtual Learning Academy Charter School is expanding their online learning experiences to include projects, internships and college courses. The school aims to create learning experiences so that students can decide how and when they want to learn the academic standards: through courses or by creating independent projects.[60]

At Gray-New Gloucester High School in Maine, students move ahead when they've demonstrated mastery of a subject or skill—not time spent in the classroom.

Boston Day and Evening Academy has eliminated the traditional year-long high school calendar and replaced it with trimester courses aligned to a system of standards-based competencies that all students master.

Vergennes Union High School in Vermont is changing the way students earn a diploma. Beginning with the graduating class of 2016, students will demonstrate that they have mastered skills required for graduation through a culminating project and by completing a number of performance-based assessments and expeditions.[61]

The Great Schools Partnership, a nonprofit organization dedicated to improving public education, has supported movement towards "proficiency-based diplomas" in Connecticut, New Hampshire, Maine and Vermont. These proficiency-based diplomas prioritize individual learning goals and learning plans that help schools and teachers design learning experiences that meet the needs of students.

Parent Perspectives

The pages that follow feature these parent stories:

In <u>8 Ways Blended Learning Changes the Game</u>, Christine Byrd describes what learning at a student's own pace means in kindergarten.

In <u>Never the First to Finish: Why Pace Matters</u>, Sarah Vander Schaaff describes the value of learning at one's own pace for her daughter.

8 Ways Blended Learning Changes the Game
Christine Byrd

"I knew that sending my oldest off to kindergarten this year would be an education for me. Volunteering in his class, I was blown away by the range of skills these 5-year-olds brought. Some were reading books and writing in complete sentences before the first day, while others were still learning the alphabet.

How could any teacher manage such disparity in her daily lessons, much less challenge the advanced kids while nurturing those who needed some extra help? Obviously, this demonstrates where 'self-paced' and 'individualized' learning get their appeal.

In the classroom, I got my first real-world experience seeing the difference between self-paced learning in a blended learning form compared with its pre-digital form—workbooks and worksheets. And what a world of difference exists.

The teacher divided the kindergartners into groups by reading level for bi-weekly Response to Instruction (RTI) reading lessons. The students rotate in groups from a writing lesson with the teacher to a reading comprehension session with volunteer parents (like me). The reading comprehension program is self-paced, with a dozen color-coded booklets and corresponding worksheets that each child must complete. Every child works on a different workbook (there's only one copy of each in the classroom), and then students trade off as they finish, each student progressing at his own pace.

For math, the entire class uses the online game-based program ST Math weekly either with iPads or in the computer lab. (Full disclosure: I work for the nonprofit MIND Research Institute that creates ST Math, and I had let my son play the games at home for months before he started at school.)

Here are eight ways blended learning is changing education:

1. **Truly self-paced.** The self-paced reading comprehension system requires an adult to keep track of who's completed which workbook and to make sure they trade off to get a new one. It's not an exact science, nor a very efficient one. A child may wait a few minutes while we figure out which workbook he or she still needs to complete and retrieve it from another student. With digital tools, this isn't an issue. The program can seamlessly and fluidly advance the child to the next problem or level of difficulty.

2. **Feedback is immediate.** After class, we correct the worksheets the students worked on. (Some may have completed two, some seven, each working at his or her own pace.) Unfortunately, there's no chance for me to tell Madison that the picture of a baby flower is in fact a "bud" and not, as she wrote, a "bit." So she missed an opportunity to learn a new vocabulary word. With the online program like ST Math, however, if a student selects four blocks as the answer to the total of one block plus two blocks, the program immediately shows that she's one block short. This helps learning occur.

3. **Teachers can be more efficient.** Another parent and I correct the worksheets. If everyone completed

different workbooks that day, there is no single answer key to check them against. Although it's relatively easy, this is the kind of mundane task that is a time-suck for any teacher.

4. **Identifying struggling students is easier.** When I later correct the papers, I notice that certain students have struggled significantly more than others. That's information that the teacher needs—and preferably during the course of the lesson, not after class. Good digital tools give teachers access to reports about how the students progress overall and whether any seem to be struggling right at that moment and need special attention.

5. **Digital is more natural.** Within reading groups, toggling between the workbooks that list questions and the worksheets used to record answers, kindergartners stumble on a surprising array of challenges, like writing answers on the wrong lines or in the wrong sections, even after a few weeks of practice. However, I watched a class of 30 kindergartners simultaneously sit down and start clicking away in ST Math the first day after watching an intro video. By comparison, this seemed so much simpler.

6. **'There's no achievement gap in video games.'** There are a number of ELL students in my son's class and one or two with learning challenges. One student in particular seems to constantly struggle with following directions in class. It seems there are too many distractions for him to focus on the teacher in front of him or the task at hand. But I noticed he remained unusually focused in in the computer lab; he was more in the zone with ST Math than I've ever

seen him. Watching this student brought to mind my colleague Dr. Art McCoy's favorite saying: 'There's no achievement gap in video games.'

7. **Games are fun.** Not all digital tools are game-based, but ST Math is; for comparison, this proves a lot more fun than a seemingly endless stream of worksheets. Words cannot express the disappointment on the face of a child when I told him that, even though he'd completed all 12 of the purple reading comprehension workbooks, he had dozens more workbooks in other colors to complete. This isn't an issue with video games, where kids compete with themselves to advance to the next level. In ST Math, for example, students solve problems to help JiJi the penguin cross the screen and "get home." This paradigm dates back to the Mario Brothers era and proves intrinsically compelling. When my son used ST Math at home, I remember him gleefully exclaiming, "Yes! 100 percent," when he completed a level with no errors. Work is more fun when presented as a game.

8. **Failure isn't failure with video games.** I have to admit, I have never been a gamer. But even I understand that there is no stigma attached with losing in video games. You simply play again, challenging yourself to make it farther next time. When my son played ST Math at home, he rarely started with "Yes! 100 percent!" He usually started with an equally gleeful "Yes! 18 percent," followed a few minutes later by, "Yes! 40 percent." Of course, in the context of schoolwork, those sound to me like failing grades. But that score doesn't carry the same meaning for a 5-year-old, nor does it with gaming. Essentially, my son felt excited to

fail a level and to get a chance to play again for a higher score. ST Math is all about learning by doing, and embracing the failure becomes an essential part of the learning process. But the red ink on those worksheets marking only two of six answers correct? I'm afraid that would still look—and feel—a lot like failure.

My few months of volunteering in my son's class have given me deeper insight into education than my previous 10 years working in the industry. One important takeaway: If you have a great teacher and you want her to spend valuable time with your student, I hope she has some powerful digital learning tools at her disposal.[62]

Never the First to Finish: Why Pace Matters
Sarah Vander Schaaff

Remember how it felt to be halfway through a math quiz when a classmate got up to turn his or hers in to the teacher? Maybe that other student rushed, or maybe he or she just happened to be super speedy. Either way, I always came to the same conclusion: I'm just never going to be that fast.

Years have passed since I've had to take a math quiz. As an adult, I'm comfortable with my own strengths and weaknesses, including the time it takes me to do particular things. But as a mother of a fourth grader, I relive those math quiz memories every time she comes home and says, "I'm just never going to be that fast." She is what you might call "slow and steady." But many of her peers—some in the same grade level and some above it—sail through these drills.

The slower pace is not usually an issue at home doing homework; here, my daughter does not get frustrated with the amount of time it takes to do her math work. She enjoys "crossing her t's and dotting her i's."

But bring in a timer, and it's a different story. I first noticed this when we worked on a website the school recommended for supplemental math work at home. I had to put a Post-it note over the timer in the upper right corner of the computer screen.

Needless to say, the Post-it eventually got ripped off the computer, some tears were shed, and even when I tweeted the company for help in hiding the timer from view, the damage had already been done. My daughter knew that the program monitored her times and sent a report of her performance to her teacher.

Then came the timed tests in school. For the first minute of these drills, students work in pencil and cannot skip around. After one minute, they switch to pen and can work in any order. After three minutes, they stop and record their one-minute score (up to their first mistake or skipped question) and their three-minute score.

Now it wasn't just one kid finishing ahead of my daughter; there were many. I was at a loss. My first instinct was to increase the things we'd already been doing: more flashcards, more drills, more online practices or working with apps. But when I considered we'd been doing the same things for more than a year with little progress, I decided we needed some fresh ideas. I wasn't going to figure this out on my own.

I turned to a tutor who had experience working with students with learning differences. The first thing the tutor said to my daughter about the timed drills was something along the lines of, "They're not fun, are they?"

I'd forgotten that all-important piece of working with young learners, which involves acknowledging the trepidation students can feel when confronting a task they find daunting. A little empathy went a long way.

Next, the tutor reframed the concept of the timer when it came to the online programs or apps. If she wanted my daughter to practice for 20 minutes, then the increase in time became a measure of that progress. Time was now on her side.

But the most surprising strategy involved how she helped my daughter learn and recall those fast facts. They drew houses for the numbers, with rooms representing each multiple. And they sang songs with the multiples woven into the lyrics.

Fast? No.

A good pace for my daughter? Yes.

It was around this time that I was able to give my daughter a cognitive assessment. I had wondered if all the difficulty and slower pace with fast facts revolved around having a weak memory. The assessment revealed that her memory was typical, but her processing speed was slightly weak.

This information helped us in a number of ways. I was better able to appreciate how hard my daughter worked and how frustrating it must have felt for her to think she needed to work twice as hard in this one area of school just to keep up. Experts says that metacognition can help students in a number of ways, but certainly giving parents and children a vocabulary with which to talk about stressful setbacks or challenges is not the least of its benefits.

Still, the timed practice drills at school persisted. And I understood the teacher's emphasis on automaticity. I told my daughter's teacher a bit about what was going on at home with the tutor and with the assessment. We weren't in the position to ask for extra time with the drills or tests, but I did want to bring the teacher on board with the larger picture. The quizzes continued. But all those songs and house drawings eventually led to a faster recall. She understood that her pace might be slower, but deep inside, she now knew she could get to the answers eventually—and that her pace was what it was. A great deal of anxiety washed away.

When the long winter break arrived, her teacher sent her home with a packet of worksheets and more timed drills. Some students might get a break, but we all acknowledged that we would be better off keeping these skills sharp. Another thing the teacher did was to frontload new units by sending me material before introducing the concepts to the entire class. This gave us more time to sit with the material and to make sure she'd become a bit familiar with it before it was presented for the first time in class.

When I write this out, it sounds like a lot of work and a bit dependent on finding the correct tutor, the right explanation for the slower pace and the ideal teacher to accommodate your specific child. But any parent who has seen a child suffer or become frustrated enough to eventually want to throw in the towel, knows that the real pain comes from not knowing how to help.

The road to finding help or integrating a solution can be filled with minor triumphs. Triumphs like the time, not too long ago, when my daughter came home beaming because she'd finished her timed drill with seconds to spare.

Was she first? No way.

But did that matter? Not anymore.[63]

Key Points

 BE INFORMED. Do the research and look for school opportunities that support competency-based learning. Advocate for these policies with teachers. Remember, competency-based learning creates opportunities for teachers to tailor their support to the specific, current needs of each student, rather than to teach to the middle.

 BE INVOLVED. Look for ways to encourage your school to adopt competency-based education. Help prepare your children for college and a future career by ensuring that they proceed through course material at a pace that is right for them.

 BE INTENTIONAL. Competency-based education provides the flexibility to master each set of skills and the knowledge necessary to meet the learning objectives of a course before students face the next set that builds on the previous one.

 BE INSPIRATIONAL. Find ways to encourage your child to move at his or her own pace in learning a new skill, whether it's learning how to ride or bike or mastering a tough concept in chemistry.

In the Toolkit

Nature is a great model for students in things moving at their own peace. See <u>10 Principles to Inspire a Love of Learning in Nature</u> to get ideas for learning outside.

See <u>tools</u> in the Try This at Home section for adaptive, interactive online resources for every age that encourage moving at one's own pace.

place

Chapter 4:
Their Place

Vanessa's Journey: Empowering Special Education Through Technology
Karla Phillips

"My daughter's story started like many children born with special needs—doctors telling us not to expect much. I did my research and discovered that visual learning may be one of her unique abilities. It's turned out to be true. Like any good Type A, control-freak, helicopter mom, I had been making my daughter watch educational videos pretty much since birth, but the truth is that, because she was still non-verbal at 2-to-3 years old, I had no idea if she was learning much. And then I bought an iPod ... A friend sent me a list of suggested pre-K apps, and I ventured into iTunes and began downloading. Some time later, we were at dinner with grandma and grandpa. I was playing with my new toy with my daughter sitting on my lap. I opened a very simple (yes, it was free) app that asked kids to identify numbers, letters, shapes, etc. What happened next forever changed how I view her educational prospects and fueled my passion and advocacy for her. By simple touch, she answered all the prompts correctly! Okay maybe one or two wrong, but enough to blow my mind. All she needed was another way to demonstrate what she had learned."[64]

Learning now happens anytime and anywhere. We have access to so much content in ways that would be unimaginable to previous generations. The invention of ubiquitous broadband, one could argue, is the single most significant innovation in learning ever. So what does this mean for our kids (and for us)? Ask yourself, have you used technology today? (You may even be reading this on an e-reader or other device.) Have you used the Internet today? If yes, you are part of the 40 percent of the world's population currently online. The next generation, what some call "Generation Z," will never know a time without the Internet; they also won't remember that people used to actually use landline phones to connect to the Internet. In other words, your child might be upset if you take him or her on a family vacation where there's no connectivity.

Anytime and anywhere learning is a term that recognizes that children can learn on their own terms and at times and places that work well for them. We explore how the concept of anytime and anywhere learning plays out in families across the United States—in schools, at home, at internships, online and beyond.

The exploding number of learning options, opportunities and choices for learning has certainly been a result of the Information Age. We increasingly employ technology to help us learn, both formally in school and at work, plus informally at home and at play. A number of factors—from the growing availability of affordable devices to developments in connecting people to high-speed networks—have contributed to an explosion of online and digital content, tools, apps and games.

Most U.S. school districts have incorporated digital learning into their classrooms and offer online learning classes to their students. Most states allow full-time online learning and have statewide virtual schools enrolling an estimated 315,000 students.[65] Including the school district-sponsored classes, it is likely that more than two million students participated in full- or part-time online learning (although record keeping is questionable) and that nearly all U.S. students have experienced some digital learning at school.

---

intentional

Advice for Analog Parents Raising Digital Kids
Carri Schneider

"Our teachers hopefully have hours and hours of support and training for integrating [technology] into the classroom, but what help are parents getting?" This is an important question posed in Educating Parents in the Siri Generation, a blog post by Carl Hooker that explores how "analog parents" can rise to meet the challenges of their "digital kids." It's this exact problem—the difference between the learning environments that most parents experienced versus the ones in which their children are learning in—that formed the basis of our Smart Parents project. Hooker, a parent and administrator, believes that schools have to be intentional about involving parents, and parents have to be intentional about modeling for their kids. He explains, "The lines between home and school have been forever blurred, and perhaps it's time to revert back to the old mantra of 'It takes a village to raise a child.' Schools need to be having conversations with parents about the digital responsibilities their kids need to be adopting. Especially in school districts with mobile device initiatives—whether it be one-to-one or BYOD—parents need to have a voice in the learning process. I'd argue that we need to take it a step further and provide parents with some level of support, much like we do with teachers."[66]

Online and Blended Learning

Online learning can be broadly defined as learning with the assistance of a computer or device and the use of the Internet. Online learning can happen asynchronously—with kids interacting with teachers and other students at different times—or synchronously—with teachers, students and their peers working collaboratively online.

Online learning is sometimes considered to be primarily beneficial for students in special circumstances—students who are home-bound, travel frequently with their families, need alternative schedules because of sports, etc. While online learning definitely plays a key role in helping in these atypical situations, online learning offers the potential to boost opportunity and outcomes for all students.

Consider students who can now access courses not offered at their school—the student who wants to learn Japanese but can't because it's too expensive for the school to hire a specific Japanese teacher, the student who now has the opportunity to earn Advanced Placement credit in biology, or the student who can take credit recovery courses online so he can graduate with his class. Where state law allows, full- and part-time access to online learning means that every student has access to a well-taught college and career preparatory curriculum. (However, only half of the states offer good or reasonably good access.)[67]

Expanded Access

Jamey Fitzpatrick, in <u>Leveraging Innovative Policy Options for Students</u>, writes:

"Imagine being an 8th-grade student living in a small, rural, Midwest community—with a passion to become a marine biologist—taking an online course in oceanography from a school, college, university or private provider located in Maine with national experts. Imagine being a 12th-grade student from a large, urban school with a desire to study Gaelic culture and language with an educational institution in Ireland. These examples are not science fiction; the ability to personalize learning has never been easier and more cost-effective."[68]

Jamey Fitzpatrick, President and CEO of Michigan Virtual School, writes, "The idea of attending a public school and selecting individual classes from multiple providers located outside of the community was even more foreign [when we were growing up]. Technology, innovation and powerful shifts in state-level policies have created a new landscape of opportunity for K-12 students in the U.S."[69] This new opportunity has created means of learning that exist beyond the use of technology while at the brick-and-mortar school. Now entire schools exist and operate solely online. Dr. Cherie Ichinose writes, "Technological advancements have transformed the schoolhouse into a limitless portal of accessible knowledge."[70]

In addition to online learning options, most schools blend digital learning with face-to-face instruction. Blended learning is "a formal education program in which a student learns at least in part through online delivery of content and instruction with some element of student control over time, place, path and/or pace where learning takes place at least in part at a supervised brick-and-mortar location away from home. A shift to online delivery for a portion of the day makes students, teachers and schools more productive. Learning in multiple modalities yields more and better data that creates an integrated and customizable learning experience."[71]

Bonnie's high school students used online math programs, online literacy tutoring, online SAT preparation and online college application and readiness tools, all while physically in the school building. Of course, those same students could use their online math program (ALEKS and Khan Academy) at home too—or in the library, at a friend's house or even while out of town— meaning that even if a student could not attend school for whatever reason, they had no excuse to not complete math work!

Online learning has now extended into the area of special education. Some students may need speech therapy, occupational therapy or counseling services. Some school districts do not provide those services, or students prefer online support (rather than in-person support). Online telehealth options can provide consistent access, flexible scheduling and qualified therapists and counselors. The online telehealth approach can also monitor and track growth, and progress can be shared with parents and teachers. As Clay Whitehead, CEO of PresenceLearning describes it, telehealth is an essential component of creating a personalized, individualized experience for kids.

"Special education is squarely focused on the individual. Individualized Education Programs (IEPs) for students with special needs define the personalized goals and objectives of the student and how the student learns. PresenceLearning makes it possible to match students with the right therapists for their situation, for therapists to develop unique experiences for their students, and for the IEP team to make the right decisions based on progress data. With teletherapy, we've proven that this is scalable, effective and efficient. From this perspective, we see special education as leading the way of next generation learning toward a future of personalized learning for all students, not just those on IEPs."[72]

Informal Learning Opportunities

Formal learning opportunities are school- or course-based and state-authorized. They are typically driven by a set of standards and assessments of those standards and recognized through grades, credits, credentials and degrees. Informal learning opportunities typically exist outside of the traditional school day or school calendar year. These opportunities largely get driven by student interests, strengths and desired areas for growth. Informal learning may also have underlying goals, but assessment in informal settings becomes more about meeting individual goals than hitting a pre-determined standard.

Building on the exceptional merit badge framework of the Boy Scouts of America and Girl Scouts of the USA, as well as reward systems common in computer games, exciting developments exist in micro-credentialing using badges to recognize informal learning. Efforts also expand what constitutes a student's academic record by acknowledging the learning that occurs outside of the traditional school day.[73] Competency-based systems (discussed in Chapter Three) will increasingly be launched to allow learning to take place and to be recognized anywhere, anytime.

The four informal learning opportunities we're most excited about are mobile learning apps, maker clubs, blogging and mobile maker apps.

Mobile learning apps. There are almost three million mobile applications available in the Apple and Android stores, plus another million in other stores. Almost 10 percent are learning apps; about half of those aim at early learning.[74] That's a lot of apps, and most of them haven't been reviewed. The best, largest, free review source, Common Sense Media (which provides Graphite for teachers), rates apps based on "age appropriateness and learning potential." It considers engagement, success with learning outcomes, opportunities to give feedback and availability of app extensions..

Mike Robb, education director at the Fred Rogers Center, suggests that adults should "take care to think about what's right for your kids" and engage "with children around the apps they use—that may mean sitting down next to them, asking them questions afterwards or finding related books or activities of interest."[75]

Toddlers and Tablets

Alex Hernandez, partner at <u>Charter School Growth Fund</u>, writes about the explosion of apps and learning-at-home options, especially for young learners:

"Fairly or not, educators criticize EdTech companies for producing uninspired products that ignore learning science and yield meager results. School officials can exacerbate such problems through bureaucratic, irrational purchasing and poor program implementation.

Early-childhood app companies have a chance to break through this logjam and lead the entire sector forward. Many developers are bypassing schools altogether and going directly to families. By removing the layers between the people making the apps and the children using the apps, developers can respond more quickly to user behavior and make better products faster. They can also experiment with new approaches to learning without having to fight through the institutional inertia of 'this is how it's always been done' or 'that will never work.'

For example, <u>Minecraft</u> is a sandbox game that allows children to flex their creative muscles by building anything they can imagine. Think SimCity crossed with Legos. While educators continue to debate whether Minecraft should be used in schools to promote creativity, the app has been downloaded 20 million times at home, captivating an entire generation of children. Innovations will continue to emerge in the space between unstructured, informal learning and structured, formal learning and, like Minecraft, blur the line separating the two."[76]

Maker clubs. The <u>Imagination Foundation</u> (where Tom is a director) is the sponsor of the <u>Global Cardboard Challenge</u>, expanding Imagination Chapters, and pop-up learning environments that encourage creativity, entrepreneurship and 21st-century skills through creative play. They use a range of tools and materials, from cardboard to advanced electronics, and can open anywhere, including in libraries, neighborhood centers and schools.

Start an Imagination Chapter!
<u>tinyurl.com/VIDEO-imagination</u>

<u>Maker Education Initiative</u> has more than three dozen Maker Corps sites that increase the capacity of youth-serving organizations, museums and libraries nationwide to engage youth and families in making.

<u>Maker Faire</u> hosts events—partly science fair, partly county fair and partly something entirely new and different—for all ages.

Blogging. Students could be blogging about their learning every week. In addition to posting to their own sites, they can blog for community news organizations, sports websites, movie review websites and online teen art communities. Posting publicly allows students to dive into niche interests and explore those online; they can then offer up their best writing to a community of people they value. In <u>10 Reasons Why I Want My Students to Blog</u>, English teacher Susan Lucille Davis writes, "Blogging is writing, 21st-century style, plain and simple. Blogging constitutes a massive genre. It comes in many forms, addresses a myriad of topics, and can certainly range in quality … Blogging provides the best venue for teaching student writing. As bloggers, young people develop crucial skills with language, tone their critical-thinking muscles and come to understand their relationship to the world."[77] Parents can play a significant role in supporting student blogging by reading and discussing blog entries with their children, starting a blog themselves (thereby modeling the importance of the medium), and creating time to give feedback to each student about his or her writing.

Mobile maker apps. The list of mobile maker apps has exploded, and many blend the best of online and hands-on learning. DIY.org has it all! Students can choose the "making" skill they want to master and have their choice of multiple activities to practice. Skills range from linguistics and bike mechanics to graphic design and more.[78]

The New Orleans startup blink blink, markets creative circuit kits that provide all the necessary materials to engineer arts, crafts and fashion projects. They aim to empower girls through positive, early interactions with technology and engineering concepts in playful, comfortable and creative settings.[79]

A growing list exists of mobile coding apps for young learners and serious coding resources for older students.

- Code.org, advocate behind the Hour of Code, offers a place to start—Code Studio—with lots of tutorials and courses.
- Hopscotch is drag-and-drop software that teaches students the fundamentals of programming.
- Wonder Workshop makes programmable robots Dot and Dash.
- Treehouse is a great place for high school students to learn web design and development on the iPad.

Do Your Kids Need to Learn to Code? YES! But Not for the Reasons You Think
Grant Hosford

"When my daughter Naomi begged to take a LEGO robotics class, I said yes because it sounded like a door to the future. She loved it and asked me to come check it out. I was surprised to find that, in a class of 25 kids, she was the only girl and the youngest student by two years. That week I researched options for teaching young kids about computer science and was even more surprised to find there were very few resources for young kids and no real concept offering an ABCs of computer science.

For more than 40 years computer science has been taught in roughly the same way. It's been reserved primarily for gifted older kids and was introduced in a very dry way. Only a handful would stick with it and discover that making things on computers is fun, rewarding and easier than you might think. I became a little obsessed with the topic and researched two things: How young is too young to teach computer science? And, what are the benefits of studying it?

Fortunately, there is great research from MIT and Tufts (University) showing how kids as young as 4 years old can learn very sophisticated computer science concepts if you get the mouse, keyboard and syntax (meaning "how code is written") out of the way (for example). In addition, related research shows that young kids who study computer science improve transferrable skills like sequencing, which has a direct positive correlation with improved reading comprehension.

The more research I did, the more computer science looked like the perfect gateway to 21st-century skills."[80]

Anytime-Anywhere Learning

We've been touched and impressed by the stories of families traveling and learning together—for a weekend, a few months or even a few years. Consider Jeff and Gail's story.

Recognizing that their son's sense of adventure was being defined by video games, they sold their business and house, bought a sailboat and set off on an 18-month journey. Gail developed a curriculum for the boys, ages 4, 9 and 12. They often studied in the morning and explored an island and a foreign culture in the afternoon. School included the basics but also responded to the students' curiosity. They learned to identify tropical fish and learned about their habitats. One student compiled a report about sharks, teaching the rest of the family how to identify them and determine which ones to avoid. They studied the weather, listening daily to the local forecast. They learned how to communicate via radio with the proper etiquette. The students kept journals, recording their impressions of each island, culture and new friend. They studied the night sky and learned about the constellations. Their imagination was kindled and grew with hours of exploration, free time and play.

Everyone had responsibilities on the boat—real jobs, not token ones. If someone didn't do his part, the safety of the crew and vessel were at stake. The boys learned technical skills and virtues like thoroughness and responsibility. At the age of 12, the oldest was able to stand his own watch at night while the boat was underway. The kids helped save two sailboats that were sinking during the first two weeks of their journey. They gave away their toys to children who had lost everything in a hurricane.

Returning to a traditional school proved tough for the boys, but the experience had a lasting impact. The family's oldest son wrote a high school essay titled: I'd Rather Do Stuff Than Have Stuff. Jeff and Gail say, "We didn't go sailing to escape life. We went sailing so that life wouldn't escape us."[81]

Slow Parenting

A growing movement called "slow parenting" loosely means "no more rushing around physically and metaphorically, no more racing kids from soccer to violin to art class. Slow parenting cherishes quality over quantity, being in the moment and making meaningful connections with your family."[82] Carrie Contey, co-founder of Slow Family Living, says, "Slowing down and connecting with each other is about being mindful of what you're doing ... These days when everyone is so busy, we need to be intentional about making space for family time. Like all of our other activities, we need to mark it on the calendar." Contey also says that riding in the car between activities doesn't count as family time.[83]

Activity frenzy in the United States has led to what some have labeled as "Tiger Mom" or "helicopter" parenting, when young people go from activity to activity and never have any downtime to play in unstructured ways without adults. While many parents spend hours shuttling their kids to and from activities, there is also a lot less unsupervised play and less unstructured summer roaming. Given rational safety concerns, most kids lead lives more sheltered and scheduled—with fewer opportunities to explore and learn independence. Kids need to be safe, but it's also important to create loosely structured opportunities to wander and create. (We offer tips for how to do this in the Smart Parent Toolkit.)

Parents don't have to be part of the activity frenzy and can (and should) activate interests and stimulate conversation. Anytime and anywhere learning opportunities can happen after-school, in leadership and community service programs and, of course, at home.

Learning at Home. Carri wondered what would happen if, instead of "sneaking learning" inside of educational games and activities, we had conversations with our kids about what piqued their curiosity, what they wanted to know more about, what they wanted to experience, and how they could share what they had learned. "The intentional weekend" was born, guided by those questions.[84] (See the Smart Parent Toolkit for 10 tips for the intentional weekend.)

Alfred Binford, managing director, Assessment and Direct Delivery at Pearson Learning, writes in Today's Busy Families Are Finding Time To Gather Around the Dinner Table: "In the midst of our hectic lives, we find one activity that really unites us is family dinner. In the Binford household, we make an effort for the five of us to sit down at the table together every chance we get. Whether at home, or at our favorite local restaurants, this precious time together provides us with a break from our busy lives, and time to talk, laugh (mostly at me) and re-connect ... According to an NBC News Parent Toolkit poll, families are gathering around the dinner table together more often than in previous years, with nearly four in five parents surveyed (79 percent) reporting that they have dinner with their families most days of the week. Even more exciting news is that the youngest generation of parents, Millennials, reported spending more time with their families over meals than did Baby Boomer parents ... It is no secret that as parents today, regardless of race, socioeconomic status or geographic location, many of us struggle with finding the perfect balance between our work, life and family. However, I think we are all united—as were our parents and grandparents—by deeply wanting our children to have access to the highest quality educational opportunities. The encouraging news is that our poll results paint an evolving picture: U.S. parents are striving to connect as a family more, are involved in their children's educations and are gathering around the dinner table any time they can."[85]

 Leadership Opportunities

Parents can foster and encourage students to participate in meaningful and student-centered after-school leadership opportunities. Take the example of the Neutral Zone, a youth-driven teen center in Ann Arbor, Michigan, where the emphasis is on providing youth voice, involvement and ownership at multiple levels of the organization.

John Weiss, director for strategic initiatives for <u>Neutral Zone</u>, writes in <u>Why Letting Youth "Run the Store" is Important for their Development & Life Success</u>:

"We start by letting youth have an authentic voice in our creative programs in music, visual arts and poetry. They not only create works and products driven by their own interests and ideas, they lead the charge for promoting and managing performances and exhibitions for themselves and others. Teens at Neutral Zone run their own 400-person concert venue, the B-Side, and book concerts put on by their peers. Teens also curate themed visual arts shows, providing a space for hundreds of teen artists to exhibit their works. They also publish books by their peers and professional authors through our Red Beard Press ... We train them to serve as facilitators in our weekly programs, with adult staff serving as advisors. Teen facilitators develop agendas, run the meetings, ask guiding questions and use active strategies to keep their peers engaged.

Neutral Zone's Teen Advisory Council (TAC) decides what programs get offered at the center. TAC runs an annual fundraiser to raise money later granted to other programs. At the end of each year, the TAC teens conduct a program evaluation and present their findings to the board.

At the highest levels of the organization, half of the members of the board of directors are teens. They are full voting members and sit on every board committee, from human resources to finance. Teens do things that adults might normally be reluctant to let them do. They help cultivate donors, hire the leader of the organization, approve budgets and discuss sensitive staffing issues."[86]

School Spotlights

ConnectED/Linked Learning schools use "pathways" to help students of all abilities connect learning to their interests and career goals. The schools integrate rigorous academic instruction with demanding technical curriculum and field-based learning. Pathways are developed around industry sectors, such as business and finance; building and environmental design; biomedical and health sciences; or arts, media and entertainment.

Science Leadership Academy in Philadelphia partners with local businesses and organizations to provide students with internships that help them prepare for future careers. In addition, students participate in weekly visits to the city's science museum, where they participate in mini-courses related to current exhibits.

At West Generation Academy in Colorado, the city becomes the classroom. Students visit organizations and businesses for courses such as "I Robot Digital Era Careers—Technology as a Backbone for 21st-Century Society."

At Big Picture Learning schools, students learn through internships and other real-world experiences; they design projects based on interests and passions.

Parents Love this Online School

Connections Academy, leading provider of online K-12 schools, released results from their annual parent survey. The results show why parents choose to enroll their students in full-time online public schools and also how satisfied families feel with the online experience.

Key statistics from the survey include:

- 93 percent of parents would recommend Connections Academy to other families.

- 95 percent feel the curriculum is high quality.

- 96 percent feel their child's teacher was helpful throughout the year.

- 91 percent of parents agree that their children are making good progress at Connections Academy.

- 93 percent of parents agree that they are satisfied with the variety of learning activities provided by the program.

- 93 percent of parents agree that the use of technology improves the learning experience.

- 92 percent of parents agree that the teachers improve the learning experience.

Mickey Revenaugh, executive vice president of Connections Education, offers three pieces of advice for families who may be considering full-time virtual school:

- **Do your homework.** There are a lot of virtual schools out there; choose the one that's right for your student, has high-quality programming, and elicits good outcomes.

- **Start early.** It's never too soon to figure out how online learning can work best for your family.

- **Reach out to peers.** Many families have already gone down the same path. Reach out and connect; these connections will be helpful to your family and can make your transition more successful.[87]

"Beyond satisfaction as evidenced in enrollment growth, the parent survey provides vital information that helps shape the online school programs we deliver. Being responsive to families is central to our mission; we take the results very seriously," comments Dr. Steven Guttentag, president and co-founder of Connections Academy. "Parents today have choices when it comes to K-12 education; they are forging individual education pathways that best meet the needs of their children. It's really gratifying to hear directly from these parents that they love Connections schools, their teachers and the curriculum—and that we're helping so many young people find success."[88]

Parent Perspectives

The pages that follow feature these parent stories:

In <u>The 16-Year-Old Coder: Why My Daughter No Longer Attends Public High School</u>, Joe Eames describes his daughter's approach to learning outside of the traditional school environment.

In <u>Don't Let a Piece of Paper Place Children in an Educational Box</u>, Carol Iles describes how online content has helped positively shape her daughter's school experience.

In <u>Learning While Traveling: One Family's Journey Exemplifies Anytime-Anywhere Learning</u>, Max Silverman and Sue Wilkes describe their family's journey and highlight ways they ensure their three school-aged children learn while on the road.

The 16-Year-Old Coder: Why My Daughter No Longer Attends Public High School
Joe Eames

"These last 12 months have been a strange adventure for me, my wife and our 16-year-old daughter, Katya. Last year, I kind of coerced my daughter into taking a Web design class at her high school. Shortly into that class, she used what she learned to customize her Tumblr page and fell in love with programming. After a few months, we found out about a program that our school district runs where she could spend half of her day in a full-on Web development class. She decided to apply and was accepted for her junior year.

The organization Pluralsight needed someone to help out with its Hour of Code initiative, and since they knew about my daughter's experience with coding, they asked her—along with me— to teach the 'Hour of Code' at several events, one of which was at the Utah State Capitol with the governor in attendance. Those events went well.

That experience radically changed my opinion about my daughter's future.

In the end, I felt like public high school just wasn't serving her best interests anymore, and it was time to do something radical on her behalf; at 16, she just didn't belong there anymore.

As Katya's mother and I began to discuss the possibility of taking her out of public high school, we also talked at length with Katya about this, weighing the pros and cons of this decision. I emphasized that high school gives you a nice on-ramp into the intensity of college and adult life—acknowledging that skipping that step can be detrimental to kids who arrive unprepared. Katya is NOT what you would call a good student. She struggles with completing homework, especially in classes in which she shows little interest.

I stressed that leaving high school comes along with all kinds of costs. She would have lots more responsibility. The teachers would no longer hound her about homework, and she wouldn't have a report card to judge how she was doing in class. She would have to either sink or swim, and most of the responsibility would sit on her shoulders. It was going to be much more difficult than any class she had taken previously. Being a programmer myself, I could help a lot, but I couldn't make up for a lack of self-discipline.

I frequently told her that, ultimately, the decision had to be hers; she needed to be sure that it was something she really wanted to do and that it felt like the right thing for her.

After she decided that she wanted to leave high school, she has since been asked to speak at two conferences, and I know that many more that would love to hear a 16-year-old girl talk about tech and tech education. She and I were able to go to five different elementary schools and give 4th- through 8th-graders their first exposure to coding.

Katya will also get the opportunity to face academic challenges, but it will be in a subject she loves and feels passionate about. So she'll have the opportunity to excel at something she truly cares about, while gaining the self-confidence to know that she can do amazing things with the right motivation and discipline.

She will also have the opportunity to work alongside her father. I think one of the sad byproducts of us becoming a non-agrarian society is that we no longer work alongside our parents to learn our trades. I am a firm believer that the influence of a loving father on a young girl proves not only far more positive than the influence of her peers, but also critical to her development.

As I pondered this decision early on, in my mind, I saw Katya authoring training courses for other teenage girls to learn Web development, building the mobile apps she wants to build and speaking to audiences of hundreds and thousands on all kinds of technical and educational topics; those visions made me so excited for her future.

But ultimately, it's about the opportunities I don't yet know about and can't predict. Once she has these valuable skills and time to leverage them, what opportunities will the world hold for her? I don't know, and that excites me more than anything else."[89]

Don't Let a Piece of Paper Place Children in an Educational Box
Carol Iles

"In our family, 6-year-old Kasey is the proud big sister of the bunch. Kora (3 years old) and Renly (1 year old) think she's the best.

Kasey loves learning. She loves playing with her siblings and using her imagination. She loves making new friends and going on play dates. Kasey also happens to be paraplegic. She was diagnosed with spina bifida and hydrocephalus before she was born.

This has been our first year homeschooling Kasey, an option that allows us to customize her education to meet her unique needs. We are about halfway through her kindergarten lessons at this point. Like most kids, she has her favorite subjects—loves math and handwriting … not the biggest fan of phonics.

Kasey's different diagnoses, hydrocephalus and seizures, mean extra learning hurdles, time constraints and challenges for our family. In addition to her school studies, she has to spend time strengthening her hands and fine motor skills, which greatly impact her educational journey.

Thanks to the Personal Learning Scholarship Accounts (PLSAs) in Florida, Kasey will be able to receive tools that give her the more customized experience she needs. She will be able to access a tablet device and educational software, which we would otherwise not be able to afford. It will give her the ability to learn on the go when she sits in waiting rooms or in the car on the way to various appointments and therapy sessions. These small tools will contribute in big ways to Kasey's educational growth. It gives our family resources to help her succeed. My hope for Kasey is that she will reach her full potential in spite of all the 'extras' she has to deal with. I don't want to limit her life choices based on her diagnoses. I want her to do whatever she sets her mind to, and I want to give her every opportunity in life to learn and grow."[90]

One Family's Journey Exemplifies Anytime-Anywhere Learning
Max Silverman and Sue Wilkes

"We are a family of five, consisting of two parents and three children: Noah, age 14, Caleb, age 12, and Rohama, age 10. Nearly three years ago, we began dreaming about an extended trip in which we would travel and see the world together. After many months of planning, saving and preparing, we set off on a six-month journey that include stays in Ethiopia, Jordan, Israel, Turkey, Spain, Italy, Hungary, Poland, the Czech Republic and the Netherlands.

With our oldest currently a freshman in high school, we decided from the outset that it made the most sense for our trip to comprise one full semester of school. This would allow him to complete his first semester of high school, miss a semester and then return to school for the start of his sophomore year.

Oddly enough, this was the extent of our initial thinking about traveling and school. We say oddly enough, because—to our surprise—as we told others about our trip, the first question we almost always heard focused on, 'What are you going to do about school?' With all of the historically and culturally significant countries on our itinerary, the last thing we worried about was what we were 'going to do about school.' We have had to learn as we go, but in a short time, we have witnessed the opportunities, challenges and surprises that come with learning on the road in several different countries.

As parents, we had clarity early on regarding what we hoped our kids would learn while traveling. To be honest, we were much more focused on how they would develop as young people rather than how they might advance their academic skills.

To us this meant:

- They would learn how to handle themselves and problem solve in environments very different than their own.

- They would develop an empathy and understanding of how others in the world live and sometimes struggle.

- They would be exposed to the incredible cultures and history of countries in Africa, the Middle East and Europe.

- They would nurture their curiosity and develop a deeper understanding of places and people they had only read about in books or in the news.

As we approach the halfway point of our trip, we are so pleased with all that Noah, Caleb and Rohama have learned about the world and themselves. They have each taken on volunteer opportunities in Ethiopia, figured out how to adapt to new, very different situations and started making interconnections between the different places we have visited and the people we have met.

What we did not account for in our planning—and find ourselves negotiating on a regular basis—is how to handle our kids' schooling. By this we mean either earning credits, staying on pace with certain courses or continuing to develop reading, writing and math proficiency skills. While we are far from figuring this out, we have learned much about how to do 'school' while traveling, without having it get in the way of the learning that we really want to occur.

In essence, each of our kids has a 'learning plan' that we developed with the input from teachers and each child.

Noah was most concerned about earning the credits necessary to stay on track and remain ready for his sophomore year. For him, this meant exploring online options offering credits that would be accepted by the Seattle Public Schools. After researching a few options, he decided to enroll in the Internet Academy in Federal Way, initially taking physical science, world history, geometry, Spanish and language arts.

After meeting with the school counselor and teachers, Caleb decided that it was important to keep up with algebra I so he could advance to geometry and continue his first-year Chinese studies. This learning plan needed to be quickly adjusted. While he is easily able to complete the second half of algebra through Khan Academy, we were unable to find a suitable option for Chinese. On his own, however, Caleb explored Duolingo and decided to take up Turkish as our itinerary included one month in Turkey. While he may not continue learning Turkish after this trip, we feel this will be a valuable experience as he trains his brain to learn and use other languages.

In partnership with her teacher we decided that it was important for Rohama to keep up with math, reading and writing. The reading and writing have been relatively straightforward. She reads books of her choosing on her Kindle and has decided to focus her writing on keeping a semi-daily journal of our travels. As she finishes journal entries, she likes when we work together to turn them into published pieces on our blog. Math has been a bit more complicated, as neither of us has been trained as math teachers. However, over time we have found that a combination of Khan Academy for learning new content, IXL for individual practice, along with parental tutoring using a Singapore math workbook and a set of manipulatives, seems to be doing the trick.

We continue to struggle with how to negotiate taking full advantage of all that we are seeing, while also investing in some school time on most days. Blogging has provided a great opportunity to articulate and examine what's being learned, while also growing and developing as writers. Each of our kids has decided that his or her writing will be focused on publishing blog posts. The combination of writing about something of immediate interest along with writing for an audience has helped them produce their best work, with minimal nagging from us.

While in hindsight we wish we had been more intentional about connecting our travels to our kids' schooling (such as having them read books about the places we are visiting), we have found that they are taking in their travels and their schooling on their terms. As a result, we have witnessed them

- Develop a keen interest in current events and a growing ability to connect them with what they are learning.

- Share their experiences and insights with people we meet along the way—each time sounding more articulate than the last.

- Demonstrate increasing resilience and independence at each new destination by mapping and learning about their new neighborhoods and problem solving travel logistics."[91]

Key Points

 BE INFORMED. Expanded technology, including online and blended learning options, increase the opportunities for students to learn anytime and anywhere.

 BE INVOLVED. Ask your students about their goals and create opportunities to learn anytime and anywhere. Free activities are just outside your door. A simple one—create a "sit spot" and watch nature unfold—exists anywhere outside or even right by the window.

 BE INTENTIONAL. Opportunities to learn in the community, through internships and externships plus Project-Based Learning, promote student engagement through hands-on experiences.

 BE INSPIRATIONAL. Informal learning opportunities abound, and knowing your child and his or her interests can help you in supporting the journey.

In the Toolkit

Read actionable <u>tips</u> for ensuring your child continues to learn if and when you decide to take an extended trip.

Find <u>tools</u> for online and blended learning that you can try at home tonight—for children of any age.

Start a learning <u>plan</u> with your child and see what happens. Find the learning plan template to personalize the home (or anywhere) learning experience. You can create a learning plan for yourself, too; make sure to demonstrate your own learning, and talk with your child about what you are learning along the way.

Chapter 5:
Their Path

3 Ways Parents Can Spot
Student-Centered Learning
Carri Schneider

"Recently I had the opportunity to learn alongside my 7-year-old daughter, as we used the occasion of yet another snowed-in February day to scratch the itch of one of her many curiosities. Driven partly by me, but largely by a friend at school, she's been talking a lot lately about computers and how they work, so we sat down together to try the Hour of Code. It was fun for the two of us to share a learning experience that we could both approach as something completely new. So many of our experiences alongside our children often involve us teaching them things that we ourselves have already experienced or mastered. It didn't take long, however, before I realized the greatest lessons for me in that hour wouldn't be about coding. What I gained that snowy afternoon was a set of new insights into how my daughter learns, what motivates her, what frustrates her and how my interactions either supported or discouraged her learning. I was floored by how much she was able to learn in just one hour—the same hour that could have instead been spent watching half a movie or playing another spirited round of tag with her sister through the house. So what was it about that learning experience that made it so powerful?"[92]

Carri's afternoon watching her second-grader work through an online introduction to coding revealed some powerful insights about how she learned. At first, Carri's tendency was to want to protect her daughter from what felt like an inevitable breakdown, so she offered lots of comments like, "This is going to just get harder, so hang in there and you can stop whenever you want." But following her daughter's lead, Carri soon silenced herself and quietly observed what happened instead. She'd witnessed her daughter's frustration over repetitive and uninspiring homework assignments from school, so she was pleasantly surprised to see her daughter persist eagerly through what looked like a set of repetitive and frustrating tasks. She'd experienced her daughter's tears when something felt "too hard" or "impossible" since she was a toddler, yet here she watched her push through really complex challenges that required her daughter to sometimes repeat lines of code more than a dozen times before finally getting the sequence correct.

Encouraging Ownership over Learning

What was the difference between these tasks (and related complex challenges) and the ones that regularly evoked tears at the kitchen table? In the coding example, Carri's daughter felt a strong sense of ownership over her learning in a way that deeply motivated her to persist, one step at a time, until she figured it out. She wanted to learn coding, simply because it was something she wanted to learn. It wasn't an assignment from a teacher, her parents or anyone else. It involved learning based on her own curiosity, her own interests and her own skills.

When kids experience ownership over their learning in this way, learning often looks different from how it looks in traditional education. Perhaps you've seen what happens when you let your son choose a library book he's so excited about that he starts reading while walking to the car, even though he moans and groans through reading assignments from his teacher. Maybe you have been amazed that your daughter spent hours without one complaint in the science museum, learning about the dinosaurs that had captured her imagination in a morning television show. Perhaps you've experienced this in your own life—while taking that sewing class or learning how to make a stop-motion movie by following a video tutorial or taking an online course in photography.

In Do Your Kids Need to Learn to Code? YES! But Not for the Reasons You Think, Grant Hosford explains that the content itself isn't always the key driver in exposing your child to new learning opportunities. As Grant puts it, "Do I want my kids to learn about computer science and programming? Absolutely. We spend a few hours a week on different programs ... However, it's much more important to me that they learn how to think and how to be lifelong learners. Ultimately these skills will give them a real advantage in a hyper-competitive world ... and they just might make something really cool along the way."[93]

Is it possible for schools to give ownership to students in the same ways we are able to as parents at home? It is!

Chris Watkins, Faculty Member at University of London Institute of Education, asks, "So what do we want for learners in our classes (as well as for ourselves as learners)? Here's where the metaphor of 'driving' our learning can offer some valuable description. When driving, we have an idea for a destination—perhaps a bit of a map of the territory; we have hands on the wheel, steering—making decisions as the journey unfolds; and all this is crucially related to the core process of noticing how it's going and how that relates to where we want to be. When it comes to learning, those core processes are the key to being an effective learner. They involve planning, monitoring and reflecting. Research demonstrates that when learners drive their learning, it leads to:

- Greater engagement and intrinsic motivation.

- Students setting higher challenges.

- Students evaluating their work.

- Better problem solving."[94]

In their book "<u>Making Learning Personal: The What, Who, WOW, Where and Why</u>," Barbara Bray and Kathleen McClaskey define what teaching and learning look like in student-driven learning environments. In a truly personalized setting, the leader (that is, your child) drives his or her own learning. Bray and McClaskey write, "In a personalized learning environment, learning starts with the learner. Learners understand how they learn best so they can become active participants in designing their learning goals along with their teacher. Learners take responsibility for their learning. When they own and drive their learning, they are motivated and challenged as they learn, so they work harder than their teacher."[95]

Learning is Personal for Your Child
Barbara Bray

"To really personalize learning, the roles of the teacher and learners change. The learner owns and drives his learning with the guidance of a teacher as a partner in learning. The learner may also seek others to support his learning as mentors or advisors. These others could be a parent, a mentor, someone from the community or even another learner.

Every child is unique. Just look at your own child. You probably know that he has his own interests, strengths and challenges. If you have more than one child, you definitely know each one is different...Teaching was designed to teach to the average, but there is no average. I am sure that you agree that your child is definitely not average. So how do you help your child understand how they learn?

- **Access**: Consider the best way your child accesses and processes information through digital media, visual media, audio, touch or even printed text.
- **Engage**: Describe how your child engages with content and concepts using multiple strategies that may include visuals, problem solving, collaborating with others, hands-on experiences and reflecting.
- **Express**: Determine how each learner expresses what he knows and understands through actions, such as writing, acting, presenting, building, drawing or sharing."[96]

Efforts to personalize learning in school settings often include attempts to boost student ownership of the learning experience. Blended learning leverages educational technology that gives students access to the best face-to-face instruction from teachers, combined thoughtfully with digital and online tools that often include an element of student ownership. These tools can customize the learning experience based on the profiles of individual learners. Project-Based Learning gives students opportunities to master important content and skills through real-life and authentic problems that are attached to their own personal lives, beliefs and/or communities.

Planning for College and Career

The data is clear on every measure of economic well-being—from employment and earnings to job satisfaction–young college graduates are outperforming their peers with less education. Millennials with only a high school diploma earn 62 percent of what the typical college graduate earns.[97]

Nearly all parents want their children to attend college, despite the steeply rising cost. A recent study suggests that teenagers share those aspirations but worry about taking out loans to pay for it. Two-thirds of respondents say they are worried they won't be able to afford college and feel opposed to acquiring student debt. Nearly one-third of the teenagers said college costs are "not worth it" and that the "costs will outweigh the benefits."[98]

Given stubbornly high youth unemployment rates, declining return on investment from second-tier degrees, and increasing youth concerns about higher education, four important things can be done for high school students thinking about college and careers: Acknowledge that this is the student's own path, stress the value of work experience, investigate free college credit options, and encourage a broad view of readiness.

Their Path. Encourage college in every way possible. Visit as many campuses as you can. But if your son or daughter decides college is not for him, it probably won't work to make your child do something she has decided against; he will just waste his time and your money. It's better to wait until students are motivated. The worst-case scenario is that they enroll in college, perform poorly and leave without a degree and a lot of debt.

In periods of uncertainty, listen before advising. The good news is that an expanding array of great postsecondary options exists for young people (and they are summarized in the Smart Parent Toolkit in Part Two of this book).

Good Work Experience. Regardless of whether and when your son or daughter chooses to go to college, it is really important to gain work experience; it will help him or her figure out what he or she wants to do—and not do—and will build work readiness skills that prove as important as what might be learned in college. Anything you can do to help identify and secure an internship or job that would offer valuable work experience is a big plus.

Free College Options. For students aiming at selective colleges, Advanced Placement and International Baccalaureate can be great options, and they may result in some college credit (although the more selective the college, the less likely they are to offer credit). Most states allow dual enrollment options where students can take classes at or from a community college and earn both high school and college credit. Transferability varies by state, but dual enrollment makes it possible to earn one or two years' worth of college credit while in high school.[99]

Broad Measures of Readiness. Rather than fixating on an SAT or ACT score, parents should encourage a broader view of readiness by encouraging good grades, a portfolio full of quality work, extracurricular participation, community service, valuable work experiences and, most importantly, a well-developed sense of purpose. A strong sense of purpose is a natural byproduct of student-centered learning. The extent to which a student becomes activated by interests that are inspired, intentional and informed (just like his or her parents) helps to ensure a young person who's motivated to drive his or her own learning long after earning a high school diploma. In other words, student-driven learning ensures success not just in higher education but also throughout life.

The fifth and sixth grades are good times to begin conversations about pathways through high school to college and career. Sixth- and seventh-grade academic performances will determine whether a student is able to take algebra in 8th grade and be eligible for a college preparatory curriculum in high school.

School Spotlight

At <u>Summit Public Schools</u> in California and Washington state, students are responsible for independently mastering basic content, freeing up teachers to spend class time on projects and other tasks that promote deeper inquiry. The model is based on four core ideas:

- To succeed in college and in life, students must be self-directed learners.

- In addition to basic content knowledge, students need to develop high-level cognitive skills like inquiry, listening and analysis.

- Students should have personalized learning paths so they can learn content at their own pace and in ways that work best for them.

- Teachers have the most impact by leading inter-disciplinary projects and other rich performance tasks that help students weave together content knowledge and high-level cognitive skills.

The Summit approach proves one of the most innovative in the country due to its use of personalized digital playlists to prepare for challenging projects. Summit's Personalized Learning Plan (PLP) software is the learner interface that tracks progress and launches playlists. When a student clicks on a content knowledge standard, the PLP launches a playlist including a diagnostic assessment, digital resources, practice opportunities and a final assessment.

As more schools shift to student-centered learning models like these, parents can continue to experiment with a kid-centered approach to learning at home. Doing so will reveal how ownership leads to motivation and motivation leads to powerful learning!

High Tech High in San Diego may be the best example of a project-based learning environment where students own and demonstrate their learning. As illustrated by the new movie "Most Likely to Succeed,"[100] talented teachers guide students to construct challenging projects and to exhibit quality work products. There are not many electives on the master schedule but "lots of choices within each course," says Rob Riordan, president of the HTH Graduate School of Education. Riordan adds, "We're very wedded to the cohort model with an emphasis on equity and diversity."[101] Students are well-known by several adults and feel well-supported. It's within this diverse, inclusive, challenging, yet safe and supported environment that students can then take ownership of their own learning.

Parent Perspectives

The pages that follow feature these parent stories:

In If Ever There Was a Kid Born to Read, Michael Harlow describes how trips to the museum helped drive his son's learning.

In What If We Replaced Family (And Classroom) Rules with Core Beliefs, Carri describes how the "Responsive Classroom" theory of student ownership from her second-grade classroom translated into helping her kids feel a sense of ownership over their family rules and core beliefs.

In Power of Play: Applied Knowledge, Engaged Learning, Greg Young writes about using everyday experiences as learning opportunities to activate imagination and spark curiosity.

If Ever There Was a Kid Born to Read
Michael Harlow

"We took our son to the bookstore constantly during the first four years of his life. What happened next was astounding. If ever there was a kid born to read, it was our son John. He arrived in a home with two bookworm parents, with his-and-hers overflowing bookshelves on each floor. Our idea of fun was visiting Borders, where he became known to staff members as 'The Official Borders Baby.' The local store named a drink after him, the 'John Special,' essentially chocolate milk with whipped cream so as to look like mommy and daddy's caffeinated beverages. We read to him constantly at home. I traveled for my job and memorized four of his books, so as to 'read' to him when I called each night.

John just turned nine and, to the best of my knowledge, he has never touched a book of his own accord. Getting him to pick up a book has caused more consternation than getting him to eat his vegetables and complete his chores—combined. For a time, we found this completely bewildering. He paid attention when we read to him. He learned to read on time. He has not been diagnosed with any learning disabilities. We learned he was far-sighted about six months ago, and he wears reading glasses now. While his schoolwork has improved, the new specs have not inspired a greater love of reading. A real low point came when we couldn't get him to read about his favorite activity, baseball. If he won't read this, we wondered, would he ever want to read anything? Where did we go wrong? It seemed like a cruel twist of fate that I was elected to our local board of education while our son's schoolwork quickly declined. Turns out, kids don't always follow in mom and dad's footsteps. Just as police officers' kids sometimes don't obey the laws their folks have sworn to uphold, the love of reading is not automatically transmuted. We want our son to learn about many things, and we want him to be a 'smart' kid, so what else can we do?

John had the answer all along. He learns by doing and he learns by watching. He loves to be a part of the action. We recalled our trips to the Museum of Science and Industry (MOSI) in Tampa, where at the age of four he picked up blocks with a scoop for hours on end. During other trips out of town, he was endlessly fascinated by various hands-on exhibits at the Columbus Museum of Art and the Indianapolis Children's Museum. Closer to our home, he loves learning about sea life by going to the Newport Aquarium and has recently developed an interest in astronomy after a class project in which he learned all about the planet Uranus. The recent partial solar eclipse and Rosetta comet probe have also fed his appetite for learning.

As parents, this keeps us on our toes and constantly on the lookout for learning opportunities for our child, preferably ones that are low-cost or free. Our library just opened a MakerSpace, and we will get there as soon as we can. We can't always road trip, even across town, to enhance his learning, so we look for ways to connect him with his interests any way that we can. We are also on our toes as guides to his learning. Ironically, our attempts to engage his learning on his terms have been very rewarding for us. We've had to rethink how we measure his learning. Instead of asking him for a plot summary, we ask him questions such as, 'What did you enjoy most about_____?' Or, 'What steps did you take before deciding to ____?' Recently, we had a great chance to look at the moon and try to find the planet Mars with our telescope. While I read about this on my iPhone, he peered through the lens. Fortunately, I could use that same iPhone to find stimulating questions designed to explore his understanding. 'What does the moon look like?' 'What color does the planet Mars appear to be?'

Questions about money led to us playing a lot of Monopoly. Questions about rules in sports led us to play a lot of checkers. He learned important addition and subtraction concepts while playing miniature golf. We are challenged to relate this back to what he is learning—or will learn—in school. We go slowly and walk him through the math. 'Why do you add this and that, instead of subtracting or multiplying?'

He has a good friend who he recently took to the aquarium. Arguably the 'smartest' kid in his class because of his excellent reading skills, the friend would constantly read every animal description and project activity in sight, while John would say, 'Hey, look at this!' or words to that effect. It became clear to my wife that his friend's interest in reading encouraged John to do the same. I hope that John's attention to what was happening also encouraged his friend to lift his eyes from the signs to look around every once in a while.

We have fun seeking out the educational opportunities on road trips and then engaging with John, seeing the look on his face as he discovers something else he loves almost as much as he loves baseball. For example, we've discussed energy sources when traveling across northern Indiana through a giant wind farm. It causes us to remember to appreciate these experiences while they happen, too, and to draw on them later for reference.

This is so much better than simply grabbing a book."[102]

What If We Replaced Family (and Classroom) Rules with Core Beliefs
Carri Schneider

"There are quite a few things about being a former elementary school teacher that come in handy as a parent of two school-aged children. One of my more recent discoveries relates to reinforcing the right things and getting kids involved in determining exactly what those 'right things' might be.

In my second-grade classroom, where I was a devout follower of the Responsive Classroom model, we started every school year without classroom rules. We came together and talked about how we weren't just a loose collection of individuals but rather a community of learners. Although it was intentional on my part, the conversation often organically led to the children determining that we'd need rules or laws, as they sometimes called them, in order for our community to feel like a happy place that everyone wanted to be. (Their description of a 'happy place to be' was their version of what I knew we'd need to create for the environment to be conducive to learning.)

So, I'd start by asking them what rules we needed; on our dry erase board, I'd list out every single item they came up with— no rule was too small. We'd get the usual 'raise your hand if you need to talk' and 'don't hit people,' then really specific things would arise like 'if you see a pencil on the floor, you should pick it up and put it back in the pencil cup' and 'if you have to blow your nose, you should try to be quiet when you do it … then put your tissue in the trash.' Sometimes by the end of the exercise, we'd end up with 50-

plus rules! Then I'd tell the kids it was time to memorize them all. And I'd always get the same shocked looks and open mouths!

That's when I came in with the thought: 'Hmm … What if we focused on what we should do instead of what we shouldn't do? Do you think there would be fewer things? Can we organize these into some big ideas and try to get down to just two or three rules that we can all agree upon?'

It is not by accident that our classroom rules always landed on the same three big ideas: I will take care of myself, take care of others and take care of my classroom community. Every little 'don't do this' and 'don't do that' fits neatly under one of those categories. And suddenly our classroom had been transformed into a place where we had high standards for taking care of our community and the people within it instead of a long list of rules that were not connected to any real purpose. We'd also spend some time talking about how approaching these rules as merely big ideas just 'felt better.'

So, what does all this have to do with parenting?

In my grand experiment of applying principles of teaching and learning in my classroom to those in our home, about a year ago, when our daughters were 6 and 3, we decided it was time to set some expectations for how things could work better to make everyone happier at in our household.

I launched a similar exercise with the girls. 'Papa and I have been noticing that sometimes we're all getting confused about how to talk to each other or how to clean up after ourselves and stuff like that. Do you notice that too?' This quickly turned into the girls listing off things that bugged them about various parts of their day. I asked, 'Do you think it would help to make some family rules that all of us—even the grown-ups—would all agree to follow?' They loved this part—family rules!

We started the same way as I had at school, with me letting them list all the rules they thought we would need. And, just as I suspected, some very specific details emerged: 'When I eat cereal, you shouldn't get mad if I eat the marshmallows first, if I still eat the other parts too,' and, 'I shouldn't have to wear long sleeves if I don't get cold in my classroom.'

The adults had some specific input, too: 'I don't like when I have to ask three or four times before you stop playing and get dressed,' and, 'Even if you're reading a book, I'd like you to respond when I ask you a question.' We rattled off a whole bunch of rules. There were, in fact, so many that I stopped this part of the exercise even before they ran out of ideas!

I dramatically presented this problem to the girls: 'I was hoping we could make a poster to hang in our house that listed all of our family rules on it. But there are so many of these rules that the poster would have to be as big as our whole house! What should we do? Maybe if we came up with ways we should act toward each other instead of all the things we shouldn't do, our list would be shorter.'

It was our big-hearted, creative, problem-solving extraordinaire who thought for a minute and then said, 'What if, instead of rules, we just came up with our family beliefs!' Yes! Yes! Yes! After all, this wasn't about rules; this was about our values—the things we believe as a family. The whole energy of the conversation shifted quickly from airing our grievances to determining how we could each act to make our home a happy one.

And while I highly recommend that anyone who wants to do this activity goes through the full exercise instead of just hanging up our discoveries on your wall, I want to share our family's list: *Be Kind, Be Gentle, Be Respectful, Be Safe, Be Grateful, Be Patient, Be Giving, Be Responsible, Be Helpful, Be Honest, Be Thankful, Be Loving, Be a Peacemaker, Be a Good Listener, Be Your Best Self.*

While this list is clearly longer than the three items we landed on every year in my classroom, we've found that this lengthier version breaks things down a bit and works well for younger kids. We've also found that, just like in the classroom, it feels better (and you're more likely to make the change) if someone reminds you to, 'Please be more loving,' instead of, 'Stop hitting your sister ... or else!'

And while these beliefs hang in our kitchen as a daily reminder, we've also incorporated these meaningfully into a weekly routine. On our family calendar that lists our daily school, after-school and social activities, we have a 'Words of the Week' section at the top where we rotate in each of these fifteen beliefs as a way to focus on one, remind each other what it means and generally boost our awareness of that thought.

When I can, I'm intentional about matching up the words of the week with current events, calendar items, etc. So when the kids were off from school for Martin Luther King, Jr. Day, for example, we focused that week on: 'Be a Peacemaker.' We focused on 'Be Giving' during the holidays and 'Be Gentle' when I observed we were all talking to one another with harsher words than we knew we should.

Overall, I'd encourage every family to use an exercise like this to recalibrate expectations and reframe the 'house rules.' If you're a classroom teacher, consider dedicating a half-day of that first week of school or the first week back after holiday break to generating a list of community values to replace existing rules. Both at home and at school, I've observed that taking this approach transforms the environment from one of compliance to one of collaboration. What better place in which to learn and to thrive?"[103]

Power of Play:
Applied Knowledge, Engaged Learning
Greg Young

"My wife and I have both taught for a number of years in progressive public schools. The last few years have made us think deeply about how we want to educate our children, allowing us to revisit how that influences our work in public education.

Both my wife and I firmly believe in—and want to pass along to our children—having a true love of learning, so they can become lifelong learners. Dennis Littky (co-founder of Big Picture Learning and The Met school) will frequently ask educators, parents and students to think of one word students use to describe school. You already know the answer—a unanimous 'Boring!' Education should not be boring, but oftentimes school can be. There is a critical difference between the terms 'learning,' 'educating' and 'schooling' (even though people often think of them as the same).

Our boys are interested in all kinds of things, they are very active, and they love being outside. With Henry turning 4 years old and Harrison about to turn 2, we see a brewing conflict between traditional school and the dispositions of our kids. Henry is currently infatuated with the following: volcanoes, pirates, construction and skiing. He can explain the difference between dormant and active volcanoes, and he has a loose understanding of plate tectonics. Harrison, on the other hand, is really into music and animals. We want to encourage our boys to follow their interests and passions, with a focus on learning and growing. To do this, we need to be tuned in to their social-emotional needs (soft skills), while continuing to support them further in their learning.

Think about the last thing you learned 'for yourself,' meaning not a work-related or formal school objective. Maybe it was cooking, a new hobby or something else. Chances are, you immersed yourself in trying this new activity, reading lots about it, watching YouTube videos, maybe even consulting some mentors or friends as experts. It may not have felt like 'learning,' but in reality it probably was. I posit that this is because of the playful approach you took, thinking, 'This is something fun that I enjoy and want to get better at.'

In Creating Innovators, Tony Wagner talks about the role of play as a stepping stone to passion and then to purpose. By fostering engagement through play, young people eventually discover a true passion, which can then turn into purpose. One of my good friends was an animal lover growing up; he interned at a local animal shelter all throughout high school and college, embraced veganism and now serves as director of a large animal shelter in Massachusetts.

Play can also foster pathways for young people to safely explore risks and take chances. In an inspiring article, we learned about a different kind of playground in England where kids build forts with old wood and metal, light their own fires and generally play with limited adult supervision. The Atlantic magazine article titled 'The Overprotective Kid' draws some powerful research together about what kids can learn by taking risks. The research points to deep social-emotional growth (aka the 'soft skills' that are in demand by companies and lamented as being absent from high school graduates).

Lastly, part of play as an educational tool comes from blurring the lines between imagination, reality and experiencing new things. Play doesn't always have to look exactly like recess. In fact, daydreaming is another method encouraged to allow for deep neurological connections to be made and for ideas and information to be processed.

We have spent a lot of time thinking about how to best use technology with our children. It is telling that many Silicon Valley parents eschew technology in schools where they send their children. And while we have tried to focus on limiting screen time with our boys, they both know how to navigate an iPad and are clearly interested in anything bright and glowing! While they watch their share of 'Curious George,' 'Sesame Street' and other age-appropriate content on the iPad, we are trying to introduce technology as a tool for creation, not simply consumption. My professional work is partly in the world of online learning, and yet I don't view technology itself as a silver bullet to 'fixing school;' rather I see technology as a tool that we want our boys to be able to use to extend their own learning. Technology has a role for sure, and we want to be very intentional in this department.

For us, all of this points to unschooling, a branch of homeschooling that focuses on students' interests. We think this is the direction we are now heading. At the end of the day, we want what is best for our children, and so we will continue to listen and support them as best we can. Maybe that means utilizing some traditional school settings, taking online courses or using some Web-based learning tools. It also means learning with our sons, finding dead squirrels and exploring teachable moments."[104]

Key Points

 BE INFORMED. Personalized learning environments allow students to drive their own learning.

 BE INVOLVED. Learning alongside your child and involving him or her in the world of adult work (i.e., allowing children to have input on family decisions) empowers them and helps create powerful learning opportunities.

 BE INTENTIONAL. Bring ownership to your children's attention. Involve them in determining when they feel ready to try something on their own, and create ways for them to share what they've learned with others.

 BE INSPIRATIONAL. Parents can play a key role in listening to and watching their students and looking for opportunities to connect their interests to activate learning.

In the Toolkit

Read <u>10 Ways to Inspire a Love of Learning</u> for parent-proven recommendations that tap into the power of encouraging ownership of learning.

Find informal learning <u>opportunities</u> and ideas to engage your child at any age.

Conclusion

When you ask parents what they want for their kids, many will say, "We just want them to be happy." We want more.

"If you accept that your true self is what your talent is, your real identity lies within that talent that you have a passion for," says piano prodigy Seymour Bernstein (whose story is told in the documentary "Seymour: An Introduction," directed by actor Ethan Hawke).[105]

We want our children to find and develop their talent, connect it to a mission and experience the fulfillment of making a contribution.

When you ask parents a more specific question about the virtue they want their kids to master, many say "responsibility."[106] We want more.

We want young people that take responsibility for their own learning—to allow talent and purpose to guide their development and extend their impact.

Bernstein says we're at our best when engaged in the performing arts because it integrates the intellectual, physical and emotional aspects of the human experience.

We want our children to build lives, work and relationships that integrate the intellectual, physical and emotional. We want them to appreciate that masters of their field, like Bernstein, value humility and exhibit persistence; they "practice, practice, practice."

The Role of Parents

From this investigation into parenting for powerful learning, particularly the stories contributed by more than 60 parents, we conclude that effective parents are involved, informed, intentional and inspirational.

Involved. Smart Parents are involved in their children's lives; they promote student-centered learning, exploring options for how, where and when their children learn; they encourage college and career preparation by ensuring that they are progressing at a pace that is right for them (and they don't feel bored or overwhelmed); they learn alongside their child and involve them in the world of adult work. Parent (or responsible adult) involvement is critical to student success in schools. We know this intuitively, and research confirms it. Parental involvement is associated with higher academic achievement outcomes[107] and fewer behavioral problems.[108]

Informed. Smart Parents are informed about their children as learners and advocates for their learning; they use trips and technologies to activate learner interests; they share information with teachers, mentors and other providers involved in their son or daughter's learning; they do the research and look for schools that support student-centered and competency-based learning.

Intentional. Smart Parents are intentional about creating powerful learning experiences; they cultivate mindsets and habits that support lifelong learning; they share intellectual curiosities and model the struggles and joys associated with learning; they spot opportunities to learn and demonstrate learning in the community through internships and service projects; they promote ownership and involve learners in determining when they feel ready to try something new or on their own; and they eat dinner together and talk about the world.

Inspirational. Smart Parents are inspirational as learning guides and role models; they find ways to encourage learners to try, to persist, to present, to progress; they watch, listen, empathize, connect, activate.

Smart Parents appreciate that every young person is unique and that each mixture of expectations and supports is uniquely adjusted for each learner. Smart Parents have a commitment to cultivating unique talents and linking them to a cause students care about. Smart parents help young people discover and explore their passions and purpose.

Other People's Children

MacArthur Award-winning author Lisa Delpit wrote an important and challenging book, Other People's Children: Cultural Conflict in the Classroom, 20 years ago. It explored the intended and unintended consequences of biases, practices and policies when it comes to diverse learners—particularly African-Americans.

Harvard Professor and Sociologist Robert Putnam recently published a book, Our Kids: The American Dream in Crisis, in which he describes the growing inequality between the rich and poor. He aims to create conversation and incite a shared responsibility about the role we all play in educating our kids. In a recent interview, Putnam said he hopes the U.S. is able to "return to being a nation where there are only 'our kids,' not just 'my kids.'"[109]

In conclusion, it proves important to ask, "What responsibility do we as parents have to support powerful learning for other people's children who come from less privileged backgrounds?"

While individual answers to that question are guided by ideology, we can suggest three ways to respond:

- **Support individual students:** Be a mentor or a tutor, host interns at work, and sponsor college scholarships.

- **Build the local ecosystem:** Our Smart Cities investigation identified seven keys to quality options for every family including sustained leadership, talent development, partnerships that support youth and families and capacity for new tools and schools. Smart Parents can join or start a local advocacy effort focused on one of these important issues, run for school board or support a youth and families services organization.

- **Advocate for equitable state policies:** Support school funding that reflects the challenges faced by enrolled students (even if it means less for your children's school) and equitable access to early learning, K-12 options and college. Advocate for Deeper Learning and broader outcomes for all students.

As parents, this journey for powerful learning has made us more humbled by the task of our roles, more excited about emerging opportunities and more committed to the conversation.

Part Two:
The Smart Parent Toolkit

Part Two *offers a collection of actionable resources that form the* **Smart Parent Toolkit**. *The content has been organized into sections, based on students' ages, to help provide meaningful tools that promote student-centered and personalized learning at home, at school and everywhere in between.*

Using the Toolkit

The Smart Parent Toolkit is divided into sections based on age and development. We know that early learners differ greatly from teens; therefore, some of the tips, tools, advice and strategies will be different, too. That being said, we believe some aspects of parenting to be truly universal. For example, Dr. Scott's message of getting your kids outside applies to any age. So we provide some universal parenting resources, strategies and tips at the end of this Toolkit. There is something here for everyone—whether you are expecting or you already have a toddler, elementary school-aged kids, middle schoolers or secondary students.

The Smart Parent Toolkit is broken down into the following sections:

- For Parents of...Young Learners (ages 0 to 5)
- For Parents of...Exploring Learners (ages 6 to 10)
- For Parents of...Transitioning Learners (ages 10 to 15)
- For Parents of...Young Adult Learners (ages 15 to 20+)
- Universal Parenting Tools (how-to tips, checklists and more)

Join the Smart Parents Community!

We know that so many cool resources, apps, videos and books exist, and we recognize that our list of ideas for at-home experiences is not exhaustive. We also know that you have your own great ideas about what works well for your children to foster powerful learning. So, for that reason, we encourage the sharing of specific resources that you find helpful across social media by using #SmartParents. We want to hear from parents about what's working, what you love and what you need. Chances are, someone else has already been there and can offer great ideas. With the explosion of resources on the Web, we also know that it can feel overwhelming to be given a long list of resources; therefore, in this section, we have found resources that meet our #SmartParents criteria. These are ideas we love, ideas we can use at home and ideas that have been recommended by our trusted parent contributors.

Try This at Home!
In each section, we highlight specific blogs and articles from our guest contributors that have been helpful in the framing and creation of this book. The "Try This at Home" section includes specific actionable resources and ideas that you could literally do with your student at home tonight!

Young Learners

In this section, you will find specific tips on screen time usage for young learners, tips and strategies for encouraging lifelong learning, and resources specifically designed for children from birth to 5 years old.

Spotlight On ... Young Learners

"As a nation, we can and should make smart investments in the earliest years—from birth to 5 years old, before children enter the K-12 system—so that children are primed and ready to succeed the moment they set foot in a kindergarten classroom. Parents, business leaders and elected officials are galvanizing around the notion that investments in high-quality, early childhood education are a proven means of setting children on the right academic and developmental path—as well as being a smart financial investment.

Parents of infants and toddlers know just how critical those formative years can be. The fact of the matter is that children are born learning, and their brains develop at an enormous rate in the first few years of life. This is the time when they learn and develop the early cognitive and social skills that set the foundation for later success in schools, careers and life. As a parent, I still remember when my children were in this stage—and the extraordinary amount of time and energy I spent trying to keep up with their incredible learning curves and helping them get ahead.

The latest research backs what we parents witness firsthand. By age three, a young child's brain has produced hundreds of trillions of connections among neurons—or 700 new connections every second. By age five, nearly 90 percent of brain development has occurred–motor skills, learning, analyzing, vocabulary, speech and other positive developmental strides–all of this made possible by exponentially growing connections. A child only reaches this critical development stage once in his or her lifetime, and it is imperative that parents and programs exist to nurture this important period of cognitive and social growth."[110]

Kris Perry
Early Childhood Education is Critical
for our Own Kids' Future—and the Nation's

Tips & Strategies

What can I do to ensure my child is reaching his or her milestones?

Kris Perry offers four specific strategies to ensure that even our youngest children learn every day with actionable tips for parents.

1. "Take the time to read, talk, play and sing with your child every day. Even the smallest interactions, especially before your child can talk back, help the brain growth.

2. Respond to your baby's gestures and sounds by talking and cooing back, and pick your baby up when he or she lifts his or her arms.

3. Build language skills by asking questions and exploring answers together.

4. Use daily activities and routines to build vocabulary."[111]

Kris Perry
Early Childhood Education is Critical
for our Own Kids' Future—and the Nation's

What do I do about screen time for my young kids?

We have probably received more dialogue about social media and technology than just about anything else in our Smart Parents series. Here Lisa Guernsey, author of "Screen Time: How Electronic Media—From Baby Videos to Educational Software—Affects Your Young Child," talks about screen time for toddlers.

"It's a question always sparking hot debate in parenting circles: Do you let your babies and toddlers use screens? For years, the health and child development establishment has advised parents against exposing their toddlers and babies to screen media. But daily life increasingly includes video, smartphones and touchscreen tablets. Questions fly: Is staying away really the best approach?

In late 2014, however, a new message broke through—part of a wave of pronouncements rooted in science that could make way for new approaches, pushing to make 'screen time' much more than an electronic babysitter.

The guide released by Zero to Three, a nonprofit organization focused on infants and toddlers, reveals the latest and most powerful example of a shift in the landscape. The guide, 'Screen Sense: Setting the Record Straight,' involves an objective account of the research, summarizing the implications via 'both-and' statements such as 'children should have lots of time for play in the real, 3-D world' and parents '[should] make screen use a shared experience.'

The science could even be expressed in a one-line mantra: Remember the three C's—the content, the context and the child. This means: Be choosy about the content—the apps, games and TV shows—that you let your children see. (When kids are very young, that content should be limited to material that you, the parent, would use to engage in conversation with your baby or toddler, such as electronic picture books, interactive apps or personal videos of family outings.) Be aware of the context; for example, it's good to talk with kids about what they watch, and ensure that media usage doesn't crowd out other activities, such as outdoor play and conversation-filled mealtimes. And be alert to the needs of the child as an individual; a child will react in unique ways to what he or she sees and plays with. She may need more limits or increased face-to-face time with you, depending on her age and what she might be going through at any given moment. Or she could have new interests sparked by what she experiences on-screen."[112]

Lisa Guernsey
Common Sense, Science-Based Advice
on Early Learners' Screen Time

What can families and schools do to protect children from the digital deep end?

Heather Staker, co-author of "Blended: Using Disruptive Innovation to Improve Schools," offers advice to help ensure kids don't drown in the "device deep end."

"One possibility is to ban children from devices altogether. But that throws out much of the good along with the bad. By the millions, children are overcoming math anxiety, learning to read, learning to code and discovering a host of other unprecedented enrichments—all thanks to the marvel of online resources. And even if it were desirable to do so, shielding children from all-things digital is impossible. The Internet has become so intertwined with our daily lives that it makes more sense to help children navigate this reality, rather than blinding them to its presence.

Access to devices does not have to be all or nothing. Instead, adults should moderate children's usage. Dr. Evans recommends using computers like parents used to monitor TV time: 'You can watch this, but you can't watch that.' This rings as true for teenagers as it does for young children. One school principal I know requires that the guardians of middle and high school students sign a covenant at the beginning of the year that they will parent their children. He believes that, too often, the parents of older children underestimate how much mentoring and guidance their adolescents continue to need, even as their bodies develop and become more adult-like.

To moderate usage, think of the Internet like a school bus taking your child on a field trip. Teachers plan field trips with care, including getting parents' permission, planning the learning objectives and scheduling the students' safe return. Yet with devices, adults tend to skip these steps, allowing children to wander off completely alone to any destination, with no thought of safety. A better approach involves treating virtual experiences with as much planning and concern as you would if your kids were embarking on any other activity away from you.

Dr. Evans also recommends that parents set the example by moderating their own device use. 'We know all about the importance of childhood attachment and good healthy childhood relationships with parents. Yet, if you look in the local park, you see children at a very early age not getting the tender, intense love they used to because their parents are always on their smartphones. Put them down, and be with your kids.'"[113]

Heather Staker
How to Keep Your Children from
Drowning in the Device Deep End

How can I turn my child's screen time into family time?

As digital media becomes more integrated into our lives, we know that the digital world creates an increased capacity to learn. We can both encourage and embrace the technology and provide limits for our earliest learners. Michelle Miller from Joan Ganz Cooney Center explores how to turn screen time into family time.

"At the <u>Joan Ganz Cooney Center</u>, we explore the ways that families use media together, the potential of games for learning and solutions for digital equity. We recently published a free guide called <u>Family Time with Apps</u>; it includes tips for helping busy parents decide how to introduce digital media:

- Talk with your child about which decisions you can make together. The more involved she is in the process, the more likely she will make her own good decisions in the future.

- Use apps and other mobile tools to help support your parenting goals. For example, e-books can make it easier to squeeze in 15 minutes of reading together time every day.

- <u>Research</u> shows that children learn more from all kinds of media when families participate too. So even if it's just for a few minutes, jump in and play together!

Deciding What to Download. No matter how many amazing things an app or game does, some of the most important learning happens beyond the screen. Here are a few questions to consider before downloading an activity for your child:

1. Does it allow your child to learn and grow? Playing games can place your child in the driver's seat and offer fun ways to foster her curiosity. The best activities build on your child's interests in unique ways like walking with dinosaurs, building a skyscraper or playing every instrument in a (virtual) band. Playing games together also provides a great chance for your child to be the expert and lead family time, helping her learn how to follow directions, take turns and stay focused.

2. Does it encourage communication? Some activities offer ways to create something together, like a video or a photo album. It's hard for young children to pay attention during phone calls, but video-conferencing apps can allow them to read a book or share show-and-tell with distant relatives. Even if you don't play a game together, your child benefits when you talk with her about it afterwards.

3. Does it connect different experiences? Apps, games and other mobile learning tools can be used to help address everyday challenges anytime, anywhere. Playing a game related to a new experience like the first day of school, first plane trip or first haircut can help children prepare for what will happen. Resources like Common Sense Media provide lists of activities organized by themes, such as connecting to outdoor activities and making stressful situations like road trips more fun.

Setting a Predictable Routine. Choosing what digital media to download may be easier while my daughter is very young, but controlling the 'when' and the 'where' can be a challenge. As much as we try to avoid it, she sees her parents using smartphones and tablets and wants to be part of the action. Just like with sleeping and eating, it's important to set a predictable routine and be consistent about where, when and for how long your child is allowed to play. Here are a few tips that may help:

- Choose situations or times that you feel are appropriate for using apps (maybe while waiting for an appointment), and limit the rest (for example, during meals).

- Provide a countdown to warn your child before it's time to stop playing.

- Set a regular time for family play at least once a week.

- Try to avoid using devices close to bedtime."[114]

Michelle Miller
How to Turn Screen Time into Family Time

Try This at Home!

Vroom activity cards offer ideas about ways to enrich everyday activities that will help build your young child's brain.

Get tips to make Family Time with Books a fun experience for both you and your child. Your child can learn to love reading!

The Importance of Playing Games with Your Preschooler provides some simple, classic card and board games that you can play with young children, helping them to build social and cognitive skills and regulate emotions.

Turn Any Walk into a Nature Walk presents the opportunity to help your child learn about the natural world.

Sign up for Text4baby, and receive texts about your child's development, ideas for play and links to videos, resources and more.

Exploring Learners

In this section, you will find specific tips including ways to foster a growth mindset in your student, tips for encouraging family mealtime and suggested questions to foster discussions about learning at the dinner table.

 Spotlight On ... Exploring Learners

"The knowledge and skills children gain from 6 to 12 years old form the basis of all future education. This is a time when children's brains are growing, and they are ready to soak up everything around them academically, socially and physically. Parents can help children take advantage of this readiness and build a solid foundation for later success.

Here are four key areas in which parents can guide children during the elementary school years:

Mindsets and Habits. The period between ages 6 and 12 can be relatively calm—a plateau between the hilly climbs of early childhood and the transitional teenage years. Children in this age range don't experience changes as rapidly as they once did (when sitting up, crawling, walking, etc.)—or as they soon will again, when their brain undergoes swift changes during a 'second critical period.'

The changes during this period of middle childhood are more subtle, yet this is a time when parents can guide children in forming strong work habits—completing challenging activities before fun ones, participating in chores around the house and finishing and turning in homework in a timely fashion. These habits will build a foundation for the teenage years, when bodies start to go haywire due to changing hormones and grades begin to count toward a young adult's future.

Establish a pattern for doing homework that works for your child and family. If your young child is writing, working at a table is best so that he sits at an angle to form letters well. Let your child take charge of finishing his homework, but if he needs help developing a routine, offer choices. 'Where is the best place for you to work?' Encourage your child to ask his teachers questions in the elementary years, when you can coach him and easily follow up with teachers. That way, when your child reaches higher grade levels, he will already know how to approach teachers.

Ask your child to do tasks that involve taking responsibility for her own care—cleaning her room, brushing her teeth, helping with laundry—and those that contribute to the family. Maybe she helps with feeding the dog or setting the table.

Friendship. Children at this time start to expand their relationships to people outside of the family. Making friends becomes of utmost importance. Additionally, children become more aware of how they compare with others; consequently, they become more self-conscious about how they appear to peers. This can be an adjustment for parents, whose opinions may not be as valued as they once were. Think of this time, though, as an opportunity to observe and guide where needed. This may not be as much of a possibility later on. Encourage your child to reach out to others and to explore friendships. Invite children over to your home so you can see how your child interacts with friends, and guide him toward healthy interactions.

Strengths. As children become more aware of their role in the world outside of the family, middle childhood is a great time to help children explore activities to find out what they like. Observe their interests, and give choices and suggestions for activities. In elementary school, children can try volleyball or drama for the first time a lot more easily than they can in high school, when the stakes are much higher. Every exposure a child has to new ideas and activities broadens his knowledge about the world and himself.

Help your child find her strengths so that she discovers areas where she feels competent; she can rely on these to tackle activities that don't come quite as easily. For instance, if she finds writing difficult and has a choice about what to write, guide her toward a topic she loves, like marine animals, for example. Perhaps her enthusiasm for a favorite topic will overshadow her challenges with writing.

Compassion. Finally, along with this growing awareness of the people immediately around them, elementary school-age children can think more abstractly and understand the needs of people who live in faraway places.

Children at this age begin to understand that other people may think differently than they do. This opens the door for learning about other cultures and varied ways of thinking. This also opens the door to feeling empathy for others. Ask your child questions about how he thinks others feel and kind ways to respond.

Build on these feelings by guiding your child to give to others, whether gathering contributions for a food drive or inviting another child who has been left out of a game to join. This is also the time to encourage your child to be compassionate to herself when she experiences a disappointment or failure."[115]

Liz Wimmer
The Elementary School Years:
The Four Pillars That Build a Strong Foundation

Tips & Strategies

How can I encourage my child to have a growth mindset?

We've been hearing a lot about growth mindset in education circles for a few years. Eduardo Briceño, co-founder of Mindset Works, provides specific actionable tools to encourage growth mindsets at home.

"Monitor your self-talk. Pay attention to your own internal dialogue about abilities. When you see a highly capable person, do you recognize the hard work it took to develop that competence? When you or your children struggle to do something, do you tend to conclude that you can't develop the needed ability or that you haven't developed it yet? When your child does something well, do you praise him or her for being talented or help to reflect on the behaviors that led your child to success?

When you realize you're thinking in a fixed-minded way, observe what effect that thinking has on you, and remind yourself what you've learned about the malleability of abilities and what it takes to develop expertise.

Become a role model learner. Children observe and imitate us. If we want them to be interested in learning and to work hard to develop their abilities, we need to do the same ourselves. Demonstrate that effective effort is worth doing and leads to improved abilities by setting learning goals, working hard to improve and making the learning process visible to those around you. Talk about the challenges you take on, the mistakes you make along the way, the lessons you learn and the progress you note.

Be deliberate about the messages you send. When we feel uncomfortable calculating the tip on a restaurant bill and hand it off for someone else to calculate, it conveys that we think we can't learn math and aren't working toward developing our abilities. When we speak about other people as smart or naturally talented (or unfit for a particular task), it conveys that we have fixed mindsets, which prompts children to do the same. When we cover up our failures or mistakes, rather than reflecting upon and discussing them, it conveys that we view mistakes as a sign of inability, rather than a consequence of challenge and an opportunity to learn.

Some people enjoy ongoing learning and growth as a source of fulfillment throughout their lives, one that nobody can take away from them. I wish that for you and for your children."[116]

Eduardo Briceño
Growth Mindset Parenting

What are some tips for making mealtimes matter?

It turns out family dinnertime matters. So, how can you make that family dinner actually happen? Here are five tips for creating the time ... and the meal from Mary Ryerse.

1. **"Set a goal.** Most research notes some type of improvement in child outcomes when a family participates in at least three family meals together each week.

2. **Be flexible.** As is the case for so many, with three involved kids in our household, sometimes we need to make it 'family bedtime snack' or family breakfast instead.

3. **Don't stress.** Even when mealtimes feel hectic or disorganized, take comfort in the fact that the simple act of regular mealtimes may be providing your child with stability.

4. **Focus on the benefits.** Reminding ourselves of past research and its results can help us stress less and remember the big picture.

5. **Quality matters.** Mealtimes have been noted as one of the most common periods when children communicate with parents, so if possible, guard your mealtimes from outside distractions. Turn off the TV and cell phones, and engage with each other.

Dinner conversations don't have to be complex. Here are a few discussion starters:

- What was something interesting you did or learned today? (Note an increased specificity that strays from the typical, 'How was school today?')

- Can you describe your 'donut' and your 'skunk'? This is another way of asking each child's best and most challenging parts of the day.

- What would you do if...? Pose a moral dilemma, such as: 'What would you do if you found money on the street?'

- What are you grateful for today? A focus on gratitude improves overall well-being.

- For more questions, a quick Web search can help, or make a small investment in a product such as this handy jar of questions."[117]

Mary Ryerse
You Can Thank Mom for More
than the Meal Itself: Family Dinner Matters

Try This at Home!

Khan Academy offers individualized learning resources on a wide variety of subjects from math to test prep and music.

Code.org links to online and local coding classes for those as young as 4 years old.

Play interactive games and learn about history, culture, animals and more at Encyclopedia Smithsonian: Explore Online Resources from A to Z.

Many children love origami! Find free, animated instructions for folding a multitude of animals and creations at the Origami Club.

Use this NASA site to learn how to spot the International Space Station as a family, plus discover current constellations in the night sky.

Middle School Learners

In this section, you will find specific tips, including ways to keep your child safe while using social media, smart ideas for utilizing after-school tutoring to augment learning, and ways to promote learning while traveling—from parents who already do this.

 Spotlight On ... Middle School Learners

"Understanding youngsters on the verge of—or already in the trenches of—middle school can be like finishing a complex puzzle, only to realize there is a single missing piece; just when you think you have them all figured out, they pivot and leave you just as confused as when you started. Children this age sometimes feel like a walking contradiction: they want your love, but would prefer you did not show it in public; what makes them laugh one day, brings them to tears the next; going to school used to be the best part of their day, now they dread it. Whatever contradictions exist in your household, it is important to remember that the journey these soon-to-be adults are traveling is a difficult yet awesome one. They find themselves in a constant state of learning and discovery, and as parents and guardians, we get to come along for the ride!

Combine students' physical and emotional changes with new school environments and increasing independence, and unique challenges for parents and children develop. Adolescence proves a time of development, discovery and transition for kids. It is key for us to better understand how we increase motivation, build persistence, support the transition into a more independent experience and prepare for future success.

As a middle school educator, my mantra was patience and understanding. I had Post-it notes around my classroom reminding me that my job involved supporting and also pushing these young adults to challenge themselves in new way, even when they made me want to pull out my hair. This is a time when they need support and guidance, but they also need the freedom to have experiences on their own terms.

When we find ways to personalize the learning experience for students, we support their transition toward greater independence, and we help activate learning. Here is what I have learned about middle schoolers:

1. **They need adults to teach them how the world works but also be conscious of how their brain functions.** The teenage brain is prime for learning. Recent research shows that the brains of adolescents have not yet fully developed; this actually doesn't happen until the mid-20s. This means that, just as in early childhood, adolescents function in a pivotal stage where it is 'easier' to learn and memorize. Teenagers also tend to be risk takers and not as concerned with the future as adults. This is largely due to the fact that their frontal lobe is not yet fully connected (the frontal lobe is associated with planning and motivation, among other things!). They may not be thinking of job interviews as they post photos and choose less than exemplar friends, so it will

be my job to help them engage responsibly and to use these channels to post only the things that make them most proud. It is important that we support those conversations and help our children make connections between their learning, their life and their future.

2. **They should be held to high expectations, BUT allowed to make (harmless) mistakes.** As a parent we want the best for our children. This is a good thing, but expecting perfection from your children will only lead to disappointment for you and your child. Outside of the school setting, learning by trial and error proves not only acceptable, but it is encouraged. For some reason, that doesn't always transition into the classroom where self-conscious students often become fearful about making mistakes. When students can make and learn from mistakes, they also discover concepts on their own and develop a deeper understanding. The same rings true outside of the classroom. I am a firm believer in setting high behavioral expectations ... some might even call me strict, although I would prefer to say I am serious. Rules and guidelines are important, as they set the stage for how to engage with the world, but I never want to enforce something that challenges my kids' passions or limits their creativity. I want to remember to have a positive reaction to mistakes; I want to teach them to reflect, reiterate and improve rather than just shut down. I want to support a growth mindset that encourages them to be confident about being in control of their intelligence.

3. **They need support in thinking about the future but also need to be encouraged to embrace the present.** Growing up, it was never a question whether I would go on to college. The idea was planted early on, and I

never felt the need to challenge it. With the ever-changing landscape of technology, the learning opportunities for my sons may look very different that what was available to me. This may entail college, but it may involve another alternative. It's most important that I at least start conversations with them about what their futures will look like. They don't have to follow the same path I did, but thinking ahead creates an opportunity to set goals and build motivation. That being said, I don't want discussions about the future to take away the value of learning for the sake of learning. Learning should feel good. And I hope to create a home environment that enables them to learn about the things that interest them. (Finding a school that supports that sort of personalization will be key as well.)

4. **They need you to be involved, AND they need to take ownership over their learning.** If you can't let go a little during adolescence, then you might also be way more involved than you want to in adulthood. When I was a teacher, the students with the most success were those who had involved parents. Involvement doesn't mean helicopter parenting. It just means that you know what is going on in your child's life. At this age, students begin testing limits and gaining a better sense of what and how they can control certain aspects of their lives. I want to help them develop their own sense of responsibility and ownership. I will do my best to help students' find passion in what they do and to model positive goal setting and reflection practices. Give them the opportunity to speak their mind, and then truly listen to what they have to say!"[118]

Megan Mead
Understanding Your Middle Schooler: 4 Tips for Success

Tips & Strategies

My child has an iPhone and is constantly on social media. How can I keep him or her safe?

Parents of middle school-aged students often start to worry about usage of smartphones and social media. We've gathered some tried and true tips from a former principal and current parent Janice Wyatt-Ross about monitoring social media.

"As a former high school administrator, I know all too well the dangers of adolescents using social media. I have mediated plenty of fights, verbal confrontations and school disruptions due to conversations conducted via social media. When my own children entered middle school, I vowed that they would not become members of the social media society. We conducted role plays around the dinner table about how to avoid conflicts and spreading rumors.

As soon as my children entered middle school, the requests for smartphones began. It's amusing to reflect back on how firm I thought I would be in not allowing my children to have smartphones. I did relent and allow them to have electronic devices. As soon as they were given iPods, the social media frenzy began. After a year of employing certain rules and consistently implementing them, they were given smartphones. They do have social media accounts, but rules and stipulations exist for maintaining those accounts.

So far, we have only had one major infraction with text messaging, and it resulted in a device being confiscated for a month. As a parent who is also an educator, I am proud of how responsible my children have been in regard to social media.

Here are a few of the rules that I have established for electronic devices and social media usage that have worked for me:

1. Insist that you, as the parent, always know the pass code for your child's smart phone. It's important to keep a pass code on a smart phone in the event someone steals the phone or if 'friends' decide to take your child's phone and hack into a social media page to post something.

2. Check text messages. Scroll through conversations to see what your child's friends' discussions entail and how your children respond. If you have questions about the conversation, talk with your child about what you've read. It is not a secret that I check their devices. I am the parent all day, every day.

3. Your child is not allowed to have a social media page unless they follow you and you follow them. Many parents brag about not being on social media because they don't have time or they are "not into that." Parents may not be into social media, but your children sure are. To protect your children, you have to be knowledgeable of what they are doing and how they are doing it.

4. Have a smart phone curfew. I collect all phones every night at 9:30 p.m. (I do make exceptions during the summer and on Friday nights.)

5. Set restrictions on electronic device usage. No electronic devices are allowed at the dinner table. No electronic devices are allowed during homework time. No electronic device usage is allowed between 9:30 p.m. and 8 a.m.

6. Social media pages must be private. Instruct your children to not post their full name, birthday, grade in school, name of their school, address, phone number or any personal, identifiable information in their profiles. They should not accept follower requests or friend requests from people they do not know. (Some consider it a popularity contest to gather more than 1,000 friends or followers.)

At this time in their lives, teens and pre-teens want to fit in with their peers. Social media allows them to join in their friends' conversations and to feel connected to the group. If they are not familiar with everything going on within their peer group, they will tend to feel like an outcast or an undesirable addition.

Children have to learn responsibility. Parents cannot do everything for their children nor can we shield them from everything. In my opinion, my children need me now more than they did as infants and when they were in elementary school. They need guidance and direction at this phase of their lives, because the choices they make can have long-lasting or sometimes tragic consequences. I give my kids freedom, but supervised freedom. Just like when they were younger, they were allowed to pick out their own clothes for school. Yes, they did choose outfits, but they selected from options I had already pre-selected. This is what I mean by supervised freedom. Their choices are pre-determined. It is okay to let your children experience social media, however parents should be aware of how to seek help when they need it. The Internet is full of helpful sites to help parents navigate the world of smart technology and social media. Do your homework. Communicate openly with your child about his or her usage of social media. Don't be afraid to assert your parental authority. Freely express your expectations of how your child should behave on social media. Help your child be safe."[119]

Janice Wyatt-Ross
Kids, Smart Phones and Social Media:
6 Rules for Success and Safety

How do I best utilize after-school tutoring to promote powerful learning?

Here are tips about what works well and how to support students after school from educator Cara Thorpe.

"Bringing educational supplements into a student's week affords parents and caregivers the opportunity to incorporate a powerful relationship element into a child's life. Adding the right model in the right way scaffolds a student's current educational model, preparing for more meaningful future experiences and independence. The good news: There is not one right way. However, in spite of our desire to immediately fill a need, extending the school day in a meaningful way requires consideration and planning. This is the fun part! So, how do you ensure the "after-school" time is a time for powerful learning?

Realize you are not alone. Connect with other parents, teachers, coaches, relatives and caregivers whom you trust. Ask questions that help you gain insight on others' positive educational experiences in the community, especially those utilizing components of personalized learning. Your search will provide valuable information on relationship-based resources in your local area and support for you as well.

Reconnect with your child. If you are considering hiring a tutor or working on a particular school-related weakness, the relationship with your child has likely been strained. Take time away from stress-inducing conversations, and find an activity you enjoy doing together. Rediscover the silly, fun-loving sides of you that may have gotten lost in the school battle. What are the ways you can celebrate your child's strengths through play or discussion?

Reflect on your current after-school routine. What is the ideal? How does it differ from your current situation? Ask your children: How can we work more effectively (or happily) together? What is the specific academic area we would like to supplement, improve or build on? In what ways does your child seem to best learn, think or achieve?

Respond to your reflection.

The program you create with your child's input should:

1. Be meaningful.

2. Connect to the school curriculum in a novel or flexible way.

3. Provide opportunity for routine, organization and reflection.

4. Inspire further learning opportunities.

5. Spark conversation and sharing in your home.

Some possibilities:

- Is there a service project in your community that could tie into learning?

- Do you know a group of students particularly interested in a specific subject, sport, language, geographical location or activity? How can you utilize this information to facilitate an academic spark? A mentor may gather a handful of science-minded students who need help practicing multiplication facts, or you may help organize an AP test study group with the goal of cooking healthy dinner together each week.

- Perhaps there's a writing assignment that sparks your child's interest or a year-long project with several benchmarks built in along the way. Students can learn about story writing by creating and illustrating their own comic books."[120]

Cara Thorpe
The Power of Personal Relationships
in Personalized Learning

How can I turn family travel into an extended learning opportunity?

Husband and wife Max Silverman and Sue Wilkes share their advice for families who may be considering extended travel with their children. Pulling children from school and opting to "learn on the road" may feel a bit overwhelming. Here are some tips based on their family's experience.

1. "Decide as a family, in advance of travel, how much time you want to dedicate to schooling on the road.

2. Set clear expectations with each child on what he needs to accomplish.

3. Understand as parents that you will probably be more involved in supporting each child with their schooling than you may initially imagine.

4. Map out when and where you will have access to technology and the Internet.

5. Find ways to connect what your children are experiencing with their schooling. This is most easily accomplished through reading and writing about places you visit.

6. Don't underestimate how much your children can learn merely from the experience of traveling and visiting other countries. Try not to let their schooling get in the way of their learning."[121]

Max Silverman and Sue Wilkes
One Family's Journey Exemplifies
Anytime-Anywhere Learning

My middle schooler is in a unique stage. What are some specific tips to encourage powerful learning for this age group?

The following ideas from Tom Vander Ark have been created for late elementary school- to middle school-aged students, but could easily flex up or down.

"Dinner table prompts:

- What did you most enjoy about today? Why?
- Was there anything hard about your day? How did you work through it?
- What's your opinion about what's happening in the news? What's your evidence?

Outdoor adventures:

- Ask children to conduct a short research project to learn something new.
- Ask children to create a photo journal and presentation.
- Go on a neighborhood or nature walk, and ask, 'What do you see?'

Taking a trip:

- Ask each child to pick a journal topic (e.g., animals, sports, architecture, characters) and report on it at the end of the trip.
- Plot your trip on the map, and track your progress using GPS. Bonus points for trying Geocaching!

Nights out:

- Pick a play or musical together, and do 30 minutes of research on the topic and author as a team.

- Pick a symphony concert, and spend 30 minutes reviewing and/or comparing the music to other artists.

Nights in:

- Pick a documentary movie, and then conduct a movie review and discussion.

Plan a meal:

- Ask the kids to pick a theme, research a recipe, build a grocery list and cook a meal.
- Write a review of a home-cooked or restaurant meal (you may end up on Yelp!).

Make something:

- Before you throw away that big box, leave it in the living room with some markers and see what magic unfolds before your eyes.

Summer school:

- Ask for a monthly blog about a book (a good excuse to launch a learning blog).
- Ask for a plan for a new business.

Reading:

- Start or join a family book club.
- Organize a 'book swap' with a friend. Trade books with a journal that explains why you picked that book to share, and ask your friend to then offer his or her opinion on the book too."[122]

Tom Vander Ark
Parenting for Powerful Learning: 35 Tips

Try This at Home!

The Big History Project tells the story of the universe in a multi-unit video format.

The video series Being 12: The Year Everything Changes shares young people's experiences about turning 12 years old.

At appinventor.org, you can start building apps without any prior experience.

Go to The Mint to learn together how to successfully manage money and to reach goals.

Learn about Self-Organized Learning Environments (SOLE) and how to bring them to your community at School in the Cloud.

Young Adult Learners

In this section, you will find specific tips, including student-centered practices for the college application process, best practices for preparing students for life after high school and tips for cultivating learning mindsets associated with college and career readiness.

 Spotlight On ... Young Adult Learners

"The brain is the last organ in the body to mature, and recent neuroscience has uncovered remarkable facts about brain development. While it has been well-known that the infant and childhood brain have a capacity for accelerated learning, we only recently have begun to understand that the brain also dynamically grows throughout adolescence and young adulthood. Since as long ago as the early 1980s, research has identified a so-called 'critical period' in early childhood during which a child can learn multiple languages or acquire rapid proficiency at a sport or musical instrument. Learning is partially a product of connections made between brain cells, or neurons. These connections, called synapses, exist at higher levels in the child brain than in adults', and they can strengthen in response to activation much faster, too. Synaptic strengthening due to activation and use—called 'plasticity'—is molded by the experience that activates the brain. This understanding that experience can modify brain development has formed the basis of many successful applications in childhood, such as early enrichment programs and Head Start curricula. However, until the last decade, it was largely assumed—even by scientists—that the brain reached full maturity around puberty. Recent research has dispelled these myths, and we now know that the brain does not fully mature until the mid-20s and that the teen brain in particular is not simply an adult brain with fewer miles on it.

These discoveries about the state of teen and young adult brains are nothing short of miraculous. First, it is clear that synapses in the teenage brain still have much plasticity— not as much as the child's brain, but certainly more than they will have in adulthood. It's often been referred to as a 'second critical period.' Hence the ability to learn and memorize becomes much easier and stronger in this age window. In fact, recent research has shown that one's IQ can even change in the teen years! Synapses peak in number during development then decrease later in the adult years. Teenage and young adult (i.e., college) brains are 'learning machines.' Ironically, though, the owners of these well-honed machines can imperil this valuable attribute: synaptic plasticity can be easily impaired by sleep deprivation, stress, alcohol, cannabis and other drugs like MDMA (molly) or cocaine. Ironically, compared to adults, teenage synapses respond strongly not only to good things, but they also can be more affected by negative stimuli as well.

Why would the teenagers put their brains at risk at such a sensitive stage? Well, that touches upon another aspect of brain development: the tendency for teenagers to be high risk takers. A major difference between the adolescent brain and the adult brain involves the fact that the frontal lobes—the seat of judgment, insight, empathy and impulse control—is not yet fully connected. The process of connecting tracts between brain regions to each other is a result of a slow insulation of these tracts by a natural substance called myelin. This takes more than two decades to complete, with the process commencing in the back of the brain and moving forward, leaving the frontal lobes as the last region to be connected. Hence why teens often face challenges with self-organization and impulse control while, on the other hand, experiencing revved-up learning. Risk-taking behavior typical of this period in life can lead to excess stress, substance abuse or other negative experiences that can actually prevent synapses from functioning normally; this can not only affect students' grades the next day, but can also adversely affect how brains will function by adulthood.

Teens prove great learners, and it is really important for both parents and teens themselves to know the facts about what this special window of development means in terms of strengths and vulnerabilities. Most research is very new, and this is the first teen generation to have the benefit of this information. After all, teens and young people are data-driven, and a wave of new facts reveal even more about the adolescent brain. Teens should be empowered by this new knowledge. Given their plasticity, the teen period proves a great time to work on building strengths and correcting weaknesses—much easier done now than later as an adult.

Parents should take an active role in modeling decision-making and helping their teens identify unique skill sets. Biological evidence does indeed exist to back up the 'late bloomer' who doesn't start to show strengths until midway through the teen years! Parents and teens should understand the negative effects of stress and sleep deprivation on the process of the synaptic plasticity of learning. As sleep cycles temporarily shift later in adolescence, teens always hover on the edge of sleep deprivation due to early starts demanded by schools' schedules. Science shows that teens, while they will hate to admit it, still remain vulnerable to the effects of multitasking while learning, so parents should help them make choices about how to focus when studying.

Digital distraction proves a huge temptation, especially given youngsters' challenges with impulse control. While the neurobiology of the teen brain probably hasn't changed for millennia, our environment has. An unprecedented amount of stimulation now exists for the average teen, coming in at an alarming speed and with a range of content that often can push beyond what is appropriate for this age group. Teens themselves need to be made aware of the easy danger of becoming addicted to Internet games or social networking; given their lack of frontal lobe influence, they can find these activities hard to resist or to balance with other life activities. We need to start an honest conversation with our teens about what they experience and, as adults (since we do have our frontal lobes), we can help them make choices about how they handle their exposure to Internet gaming, social networking and other on-demand activities.

As a parent, knowing why your teen behaves a certain way is part of maintaining your own balance; this should decrease frustration and anger levels, so that parents remain connected and less alienated from their teens. It's actually not a time to 'suffer' through; instead, it's a time of wondrous change in your child—one of celebration and also fleeting opportunities that will form the scaffold for the brain your children will use for the rest of their lives."[123]

Dr. Frances Jensen
The Teenage Brain:
Scaffolding the Brain for Lifelong Learning

Tips & Strategies

How can I put the college process into my student's hands?

The teen years prove critical to the planning of college and future careers. Here are some great strategies to help parents make the most of this time from Carol Barash, founder of Story2.

"The payoffs for this approach are huge; your child will learn how to manage a big, complex project, they will land at a college that is right for them and—most importantly— you will be able to enjoy your child's last year at home as a parent and advisor, not their project manager.

1. **Listen to your child.** When students are ready, they will start to organize their own college process. It may be chaotic at first. So learn to ask questions, and then listen. Instead of saying, 'You should…', 'You really need to…', or 'How can I help you…?' try, 'Can you tell me a little more about that?' 'What did you learn?' or 'What things you are you doing now that you really want to be doing next year?'

2. **Focus on fit.** Before worrying about specific colleges, help your child to identify the characteristics of colleges in which they will best learn and thrive. Do they want a very structured academic program or a lot of choices? Are they an auditory, visual or kinesthetic learner? What type of community will best nurture his or her spirit?

3. **Remember the higher education landscape is changing rapidly.** College is still your child's best path to professional access and success, but 'college' is shifting into a wide range of different pathways. Help your child consider the widest range of options—not just for the first step, but a lifetime of learning … in and out of work.

4. **Keep standardized tests in perspective.** Help your child to figure out which standardized tests they need to take, prepare for them and then get them done. Many students keep taking tests again and again, rather than focusing on other parts of their studies and college planning.

5. **Talk about money.** Students worry about how they will pay for college. Make it easier by being very clear with them about how much you can pay and how much they will need to earn (scholarships) or borrow (loans) to complete college. Don't guess about these numbers! Every college is required to have a net price calculator (and FAFSA has one), so your child can calculate the real cost of attending a particular college based on his or her academic profile and your income.

6. **Encourage independence.** When your teenager has one of those 'Mommy, I love you so much … will you do this for me?' baby-face moments, hug them, remind them you love them, too, and then let them get on with the work at hand. Encourage them to push beyond the requirements of their classes to pursue what they really love; encourage them to try new things; encourage them to disagree with you and honor them when they do. This will prove much more fun than fighting.

7. **Nurture problem solving.** If they bring their problem to you, be happy that they trust you enough to share it, but remember it is not your job to fix every dilemma! When your children get stuck, help them develop a framework for making their own decisions. If they are juggling too much and drowning, encourage them to choose what really matters most, to do fewer things and do them better.

8. **Make the journey fun.** Make your kitchen table and living room places your child looks forward to, not the 'college-planning war zone' they dread. Make your car a 'college-free zone' and talk about other things. At least once a week, take a walk with your child and follow the conversation wherever it leads.

9. **Take care of yourself.** Do whatever it takes to keep yourself balanced and nimble: eat healthy foods, sleep consistently, exercise and meditate. And try not to talk about college with other parents. It just doesn't help. It often gets filtered back to the students, fostering competition and stress. (If you find yourself constantly discussing the topic, perhaps you want to apply to college or graduate school for yourself.)

10. **No matter what, don't do the work for them!** This is the most important thing to remember. Really. If your child is not ready to complete the college application process, they are not ready for college. But they likely *are* ready, so love them for the chaotic, risk-prone creatures that adolescents tend to be; meanwhile, you be the person who provides relief from the college stress surrounding them.

Think of it this way: In your child's last year of high school, you are building the foundations for parenting them after they leave home. Be a resource they return to—someone who helps figure out where they are going and remains available to gently guide them past the inevitable bumps they'll encounter along that journey. It's not easy to step back, but the payoffs prove immense and long-lasting."[124]

Carol Barash
10 Things Parents of High School Juniors
Should Start Doing Now

How can I encourage my child to get a head start on the college process?

If you're a parent of a high school junior (or will be one day), you can encourage these students to begin collecting the information they will need to apply to and get accepted at one or more colleges that seem to be a good match both academically and financially. Here are some tips for getting a running start.

1. **"Encourage your student to visit one or more colleges.** Simply visiting colleges or universities near your home can give you a sense of what to expect. Ideally, visit a large university, a small college and a mid-sized school. Walk around the campus, visit the bookstore, amble through a few academic buildings, and have lunch in the student center. Talk to students and ask them what they like most about their college experience. This investment of a couple Saturday afternoons will provide you with valuable perspectives on what to expect as you begin searching for the ideal college.

2. **Encourage your student to think broadly about what they desire from a college.** While selecting a major is a good place to start, students should consider other important variables including the size of the college and the classes, the makeup of the student body, the availability of extracurricular activities that match their interests, their comfort level within the community in which the college is located and, of course, the financial support available.

3. **Encourage students to take both the ACT and the SAT.** Seriously, take both the ACT and the SAT, as most colleges accept both tests. Bear in mind that some highly-selective colleges may require students to take SAT subject tests. And, yes, it is important to prepare for the tests, but students don't have to choose a high-cost, test-prep program. A wide range of test-prep options exist, ranging from those that cost less than $25 to those topping $1,000-plus.

4. **Talk about money with your child.** Now is the time to get a grip on the likely costs of the colleges you are considering. Begin with a conversation about what you can afford. However, don't look at each school in terms of what the website lists as the annual bill for tuition, room and board. Doing so won't necessarily give you an accurate picture of what you are likely to pay. Use a Net Price Calculator such as the one on College Raptor to obtain an estimated financial aid package for the four-year colleges that most interest you. Be sure to take into account your family's financial circumstances. This will give you a much clearer picture of the actual cost of attending a college after grants and scholarships have been applied.

5. **Have your student build a realistic list of top 10 schools.** Then, your child can make a realistic timeline for completing every step of the college application process.

6. **Encourage your child to do something.** Suggestions include: Get outside of the classroom and do something. When asked on a college application or in an interview what you like to do, it will be hard to put a positive spin on playing video games or hanging out

with friends, so contribute to the world around you. If you play an instrument, round up some musical friends and organize concerts at a senior center. If you are an athlete, collect gently-used sports equipment to donate to kids in a third-world country or the inner city of your own hometown. Applications submitted by solid students are commonplace at a lot of schools. Seven out of 10 applicants might be perfectly capable of doing the work at the school you want to attend, so college admissions officers will be looking to admit students who can further contribute to their college community."[125]

Richard Ferguson
Sage Advice From a Higher Ed Veteran:
Getting a Head Start on Finding the Right College

What experiences help prepare students for life after high school?

By experiencing success while in high school, students gain valuable knowledge, skills and dispositions. Tom brings us 15 experiences every high school student deserves. If it doesn't look like they will be given these experiences in school, then make them a priority during family time.

1. "Enjoyment of high-quality challenging literature.

2. Success reading and writing technical and informational texts.

3. Calculating probabilities and using algebraic thinking to solve problems.

4. Conducting scientific investigations and reporting results to public audiences.

5. Producing a professional-quality publication and multimedia presentation.

6. Making and coding things of which they feel proud.

7. Gaining positive and challenging work experiences in several settings.

8. Experiencing the rewards of community service.

9. Participating in visual and performing arts.

10. Attaining world-language fluency.

11. Demonstrating personal wellness.

12. Completing a course online.

13. Building a brand and selling a product.

14. Being exposed to teamwork and project management.

15. Earning college credit—on campus if possible."[126]

Tom Vander Ark
<u>Parenting for Powerful Learning: 35 Tips</u>

What skills, habits of mind and conditions are important for success in college and career?

Learning science researchers have spent a lot of time in the last two decades shoring up why some students graduate from college and others don't. It turns out, SAT scores aren't big predictors of success in college and GPA is—but maybe not for the reasons you think. Here, Bonnie summarizes some of the research around habits of mind and conditions that are important for success in college and career.

"William Sedlacek, director of the counseling department at University of Maryland, partnered with the Gates Millennium Scholars Program (GMSP) in the early 2000s to study what attributes prove predictors of college-degree attainment for students of color. (Slightly less than half of students who start college don't finish, so the GMSP wanted to figure out why some students stay in college while others drop out.) Through his research, Sedlacek found eight attributes, or non-cognitive competencies (NCCs), that were higher predictors of success in college than either GPAs or SAT/ACT scores.

In addition to forming the basis of the GMSP application, these competencies are also used in high schools and by colleges for admissions, scholarship programs and applications.

The eight non-cognitive competencies are:

- Positive Self-Concept

- Realistic Self-Appraisal

- Skills at Navigating Systems and Understanding and Dealing with Discrimination

- Preference for Long-Range Goals over Short-Term or Immediate Needs

- Availability of a Strong Support Person

- Successful Leadership Experience

- Demonstrated Community Service and Involvement

- Knowledge Acquired in or about a Field

Schools can and should be designed with these competencies in mind, since they prove strong predictors of success in college and career—and especially for students of color. If we want to close the achievement gap, addressing the non-cognitive competencies can help create more equitable education institutions. Given their strong predictability of success in college and career, we need school leaders who incorporate these competencies into secondary programs and measure them. Simply measuring test scores is not enough, since we know these competencies matter for college and career success.

How can you help foster these competencies in your child?

- Encourage students to get out of the building to learn about fields of interest.

- Help students cultivate meaningful leadership experiences, and validate leadership experiences they already have.

- Support students in having meaningful experiences that help them cultivate skills related to real-world interests

- Encourage your student to find other adult mentors.

- Help your child talk about strengths and struggles without fear or judgment.

- Provide opportunities for students to regularly set short- and long-term goals related to their own personal visions.

- Help students navigate systems and help them recognize when certain systems seem to be unfair, unjust and stacked against them.

- Teach students not to self-bully but instead to build a positive self-concept based on a realistic sense of one's own strengths and struggles."[127]

Bonnie Lathram
8 Noncognitive Competencies for College
and Career Readiness

How can I encourage my student to learn more about the world of careers?

If you are thinking about having existential conversations with your teenager about what they may do with the rest of his or her life, point them to the <u>Roadtrip Nation</u> site and consider buying their 2015 book <u>Roadtrip Nation: A Guide to Discovering Your Path in Life.</u>

"When you became a parent, you were entrusted with a squishy little bundle of brains, possibilities and aspirations, and you committed to giving your offspring everything at your disposal and more. Now that it's time for the inevitable 'What do you want to do with life?' conversation, things aren't quite as simple as when your little one wanted to choose between being a ballerina or a lion.

You want to support your child's budding dreams (even if it doesn't involve becoming president like you'd hoped!), but it's hard to resist the urge to herd them in the direction you think would be best. What's more, society tends to reduce the breadth of career options to mass-produced molds like lawyer and electrician, making it hard to show your student options that are achievable with invention, like 'adventure tourism consultant' or 'scientist who creates jelly bean flavors.'

So, how can young people envision more possibilities and find meaningful work? (Work that's meaningful to them—not just something you'd be proud to boast about at Thanksgiving!) After interviewing thousands of professionals, we here at <u>Roadtrip Nation</u> have found one commonality among people who are the happiest with their work: They didn't follow an occupation.

1. **They followed their interests.** They took what excited them—be it reality TV or genetics—and fashioned a fulfilling way to pay the bills. Below, find ways you can help your student do the same.

2. **Urge students to let go of expectations and preconceived notions (while you do the same).** The surroundings we grew up in often act as blinders, showing us only what's within sight and masking what's beyond. Some students might believe they can only become doctors, while others might believe they could never become doctors. The key involves showing them that other career possibilities exist beyond their immediate scope—and beyond their present-day reality—ranging from sports journalism and chocolate-making to sci-fi-like space exploration.

3. **Take a long look in the mirror at your beliefs.** You likely nurse ideas about what you think your student 'should' do. But just because you've happily carried on the legacy of your family business doesn't mean your child wants to, too. Refrain from imposing your own ideals, and foster an exploration of interests (not specific careers). Finally, be prepared for surprises; your child might have declared a desire to be a Supreme Court justice when 5 years old, but things often change.

4. **Help students define what they actually want—not what others want for them.** Many people go through their entire educational and career journeys without

ever asking themselves tough questions about whether they're headed in a direction they really want to go, or whether they're just going through the motions. These conversations can feel daunting, but you can minimize the weight by packaging them into casual conversations about students' interests and hopes.

Whether you're in the car or passing the potatoes, pose neutral questions such as:

- If you could take any class, what would you take?

- If you could do anything you wanted for a day, what would you do?

- What's your favorite thing about school?

Conversations are a two-way street, so reciprocate with your reflections about your own interests, how you incorporate them into your everyday and work life and what you would have done differently in your own career now that you've gained the perspective of hindsight."[128]

Alyssa Frank and Katrina Waidelich
Doctor, Lawyer, Camel Rancher?
Helping Your Kids Discover Careers They Love

When do we start talking about and planning for college?

Discussion about college can't start too early, writes Tom Vander Ark below. Children should experience a positive presupposition that they will attend college. That idea starts at the dinner table and gets reinforced by campus visits. Taking middle-school courses, particularly in math, proves key for college readiness. Success in 6th- and 7th-grade math sets up students for success in Algebra in 8th grade, which creates the opportunity for advanced math in upper grades and a shot at a selective college.

It's increasingly possible to complete high school and college in six years, but it requires planning and preparation. It may also preclude attending a highly-selective university. Good work experience during high school is more important than ever—both paid positions as well as job-shadowing opportunities and internships. A career and technical education can be a great way to gain valuable work skills and experience as well as to secure college credits.

Selective path. Developing a four-year transcript including advanced coursework, service learning and work experiences proves critical to having the chance to attend a selective university.

Fast path. Most states allow dual enrollment options where students can take classes at or from a community college and earn both high school and college credit. Transferability varies by state, but dual enrollment makes it possible to earn one or two years' worth of college credit while in high school.

Career and technical education. Gaining a career certificate in high school can lead to good-paying jobs and scholarships for higher ed. We saw great examples of this at RAMTEC in northern Ohio where a couple young men could finish degrees with $50,000 in the bank rather than $50,000 in debt. Rather than thinking about higher education as a one-time event after high school, in a growing number of fields, a sequence of credentials can be earned throughout a career.

There are an increasing number of career and technical training programs available to high school students that combine work experience, job certificates and college credit opportunities. For example, GPS Education Partners in Wisconsin combines manufacturing work experience, high school completion and college credit opportunities.

Good work experience. Anything you can do to help identify and secure an internship or job that would provide valuable work experience is a big plus. Teens can check out Steve Blank's course on Udemy as a great resource to learn more.[129]

Tom Vander Ark
Your Kid Just Said He's Not
Going to College, Now What?

Try This at Home!

The 10 Best Online Resources for College Applications can help your child explore different colleges, strategize about how to gain admission to favorite options and find aid sources to help pay college costs.

Is your child looking for career direction? Subscribe to the Interview Archive at Roadtrip Nation to watch videos of people in a broad range of jobs describe their career path.

Your child can answer an SAT question of the day plus find practice tests at the SAT page on the College Board website.

Explore colleges and read reviews from current students at Niche, formerly College Prowler.

Learn to code for free with interactive lessons at Codeacademy.

Find out the job outlook and average pay for different careers at the Bureau of Labor Statistics.

U.S. News & World Report: Education ranks colleges to help your child find the best fit.

The Huffington Post: College Alternatives describes paths to career success based on alternative options.

Paying for college can be tough. Parents and students can check out Money magazine's article: 7 Legal Ways to Squeeze More College Aid from the FAFSA.

2U is a consortium of colleges offering online degrees.

Universal Parenting Resources, Checklists & More

In this section, you will find parenting resources for parents of students of all ages, including a checklist to determine whether your child's school is student-centered, a guide to creating a learning plan at home, a sample learning plan template and lots of ideas from parents on ways to motivate and inspire a love of learning.

Is Your Child's School Student-Centered? A Checklist for School Visits

This checklist is for parents who want to ensure that their child's school is student-centered. A student-centered classroom and establishment helps create deeper levels of engagement through a more personalized learning environment and allows for learners to thrive—by putting them in the driver's seat.

"Whether it's a neighborhood, district, public, private or charter school, parents often want to tour a potential school to see firsthand the environment and culture, as a way to inform their decisions. Your children will attend their school every day, so checking it out in advance, rather than basing opinions on a reputation or what you can learn online, can make you feel more confident about the place where your child will spend the bulk of his time. But if you can't visit your child's school ahead of time, don't worry; it's never too late. You can schedule a visit after your child has already enrolled.

How can you tell if the school you are visiting—or the school your child currently attends—is a student-centered school?

Look for:

- Students working at their own stations—choosing where to learn based on what works best for them.

- Students working at their own pace; for example, one student may be much farther ahead than another student in math. The teacher has classroom management strategies for handling the differentiation.

- Students' work is visible in the classroom and hallways, and all students are represented.

- Objectives or lesson plans are visible. Many students are visual learners, so the classroom appears to be organized. It is clear what students are doing and working on.

- Students do the bulk of the work and the talking. (In other words, don't be afraid of a loud classroom.)

- Students working on various projects; they are doing hands-on, real work.

- Students using technology to learn more about their own interests or to move at their own pace.

- A mission or vision statement for the school is visible somewhere in the building.

- There is a high degree of student engagement, which looks like enthusiasm, excitement and passion. (If you see a lot of bored students, it's probably a good idea to ask why.)

- There is a strong sense of school community. The students help one another and act respectfully and in a caring way toward one another.

- Adults are talk to each other respectfully and learn from one another. Adults model the ways students behave. If the adults seem to be having fun, connecting and learning from one another, the students will too.

- Are the kids having fun? If there's no joy, there's no learning.

After doing your observation, you will hopefully have a chance to ask some questions. Here's a handy list of questions that can guide you in learning more about the school and its student-centered approaches:

- **Parent involvement.** As a parent, would you be involved and meeting with the teacher and your child regularly (at minimum, three to four times a year) to discuss your child's academic and social-emotional growth?

- **Mentorships.** Are there opportunities for your child to be both mentored by older students and to mentor younger students?

- **Real-world learning.** How well does the school incorporate the real world and encourage meaningful real-world experiences?

- **Community involvement.** Are students involved in clubs and organizations after school that they feel passionate about? How does the school help students build connections to one another?

- **Technology.** How does the school incorporate technology to allow students to learn at their own pace?

- **Student assessment, feedback and growth.** Does assessment and feedback go beyond test scores? How does the school ensure that all students are aware of their own strengths and struggles? How does the school talk to students about their strong points and growth areas? How does the school involve parents in those conversations? Is this done in a way that is non-threatening and builds on the positives instead of derailing confidence?

- **Noncognitive skills.** In what ways do students also gain noncognitive skills at the school—skills, attributes and habits of mind that go beyond reading, writing and math?

- **Discipline.** How does the school handle discipline? Is there a rush to suspend students, or does the school actively teach conflict resolution and restorative justice, so students can learn how to resolve conflicts, own their mistakes and ultimately stay in school."[130]

Bonnie Lathram
Is Your Child's School Student-Centered:
A Checklist for School Visits

Creating a Learning Plan at Home

Throughout the book, we share stories about how parents empower their children and co-create student-centered learning environments so that students can have a personalized learning plan, move at their own pace, learn anytime and anywhere and drive their own learning. Start now, and you and your student can create a learning plan at home. See the template below to begin today!

Creating a learning plan with your child could also look as simple as asking them, at any age: "What do you want to know more about?" "How can you get there?" "How will you know you've learned it?"

For example, let's say your child wants to learn coding. Perhaps she heard some students talking about it at school.

Here's what a simple learning plan could look like at home:

What do you want to know more about?
Coding. I'd love to be able to make characters move on this game I heard about at school called The Foos.

How can you get there?
The company behind The Foos is codeSpark, where I can learn more, and there's also Hour of Code and groups that I could join such as CoderDojo.

How will you know you've learned it?
I really want to be able to get through a few levels of The Foos, and I want to be able to make those characters jump, duck, run and play!

Once your student has accomplished his or her goals (she's mastered a few levels of The Foos), she's ready to set another goal based on a different personal interest. This same template could be used for the whole family.

We've seen examples of how parents have gotten super creative with student learning plans. One father we know leaves QR codes with fun assignments on the refrigerator. When he gets home from work, he asks his kids if they have done the assignment—always something that is related to their interests and also educational! Creativity is king, and the sky's the limit. Creating a learning plan models and activates curiosity and can be used by students and adults.

Sample Learning Plan Template
This is a basic template that can be expanded or modified to use with your student immediately. Use the questions above as a guide, the template below (or create your own) and get started today.

Learning Plan

Student name:_____

Today's date:_____

Learning plan for quarter (circle):

Spring Summer Fall Winter

Step 1: Complete the learning plan below.

Project Title & Description
Give your work a cool title that will help you remember it, and then describe your work.

Objectives
Describe overall goals for the work. What do you hope to learn?

Essential Questions
What questions do you have, and what specifically do you want to know more about? List them here.

Resources
List up to five resources that will help you do your work.

Assessment
How will you know when your work is done? Who will evaluate you? How long will it take? Set a goal for project completion.

Step 2: For each project, create a realistic timeline for completion.

Step 3: Make sure someone holds your student accountable to the timeline and projects that he sets out to accomplish.

Step 4: Allow time for the work. Encourage the student to work on projects during downtime, and get in on the action with him or her.

Step 5: Help the student prepare for his or her demonstration of learning. This could be a video, website, blog, photo gallery, play, song—the sky's the limit. Ask questions, and encourage the student to reflect on the project's successes, strengths and areas for improvement.

Step 6: Part of the project completion could be asking your child to write a reflection as a way of processing his or her own learning. Encourage that step by modeling the way. Think of a big project you just completed, and show your child how you might reflect on that project's successes and what you learned from the work.

Step 7: Start again with a new project. Is it time to update the learning plan? One key to success involves keeping the learning plan a "live" document that is regularly updated.

Reminder for parents:

Have a discussion with your child if it's time to stop or "kill" a project. Students may start projects and then decide they are uninterested and want to move on to something else. As a parent, you can have conversations with them about this. Is it OK to quit the piano lessons to start playing the recorder? Or do you let them leave the cross-country team because they don't like the coach? Encouraging your student to finish what they start is important, but maybe not at the expense of being miserable, uninterested and unengaged. The bottom line is getting them to commit to some projects that are of interest and following those projects through to completion. We know this works, as we've seen countless examples in our own kids and with our students. Ultimately, we want students to feel great about managing their own work and goals and to feel ownership over their own learning experience![131]

Informal Learning Opportunities

Learning can happen in a variety of places. Here's a sample of ways learning might happen at home or out in the community.

Informal Learning Opportunities	
Internships	LinkedIn, Internships.com, LookSharp, National Conference of State Legislatures, Indeed
Community Involvement/ Community Service	VolunteerMatch.org, 50 Community Service Ideas for Teen Volunteers, DoSomething.org, Idealist
Maker Spaces	The Maker Map, Makerspace Playbook
Virtual Field Trips	Google Expeditions, 20 Wonderful Online Museums and Sites for Virtual Field Trips to Use in Class, Get Outta Class with Virtual Field Trips
MOOCs	Coursera, Udacity, edX
Interactive Websites and Games	Great Websites for Kids sponsored by the American Library Association, San Francisco's Exploratorium, PBS Kids
Camps/Programs	Close Up, Camp Kennedy Space Center and Space Camp
Study/Volunteer Abroad	Amigos de las Americas, Cross-Cultural Solutions, Bureau of Educational and Cultural Affairs

Making School Choices
that are Right for your Child

Gary Gruber, author of "Your Child, Your Choice: Finding the Right School for Your Child," writes about what parents really want from schools and how to make informed decisions about a child's education.

"As parents, you have more school choices available now than at any time in recent history. There are traditional public schools, usually part of a larger district that range from very large urban districts to smaller and more affluent suburban districts. Some are rural districts with only one, two or three schools. There are charter schools, public schools of choice, entry to which is often by lottery. There are magnet schools, pilot schools, alternative schools and special needs schools. There are nonprofit, independent schools, funded largely by tuition; faith-based schools which comprise the majority of private schools; proprietary, for-profit schools owned and managed by an individual or a larger corporation.

The challenge involves determining how to make an informed choice that includes the age and stage of your child and his or her specific needs and interests. It is reasonable to expect that most children have the capacity to develop the skills and to acquire an education that will help them be productive members of a community as well as happy and successful individuals. It is also incumbent upon parents to zero in on their child's strengths and capitalize on those to help develop the hidden talents that exist within every child.

The educational journey needs to have a vision that extends beyond one year or even four years and includes many experiences beyond the walls of a school. Parents do not need to be too concerned about short-term effects because learning is cumulative over time, and education is a process, not an event.

What most parents seem to want, regardless of where they live or their socio-economic status, is exemplified by a quote from a film, 14 years in the making. 'American Promise,' by Michele Stephenson and Joe Brewster, documents their son's and his best friend's educational experiences at an elite private school in New York City:

'... Parents want their children to acquire a sense of self-esteem and self-determination. And every permutation of the academic experience (single sex/coed, public/private/charter, racially diverse and downtown or socioeconomically stratified uptown) is presented as some grand experiment that might reveal 'The Solution' to growing exceptional children, as if such a thing exists.'

As parents you want your children to be motivated, to be engaged in meaningful learning experiences and to have solid relationships with their teachers that are positive, supportive and inspiring. You want your children to be able to relate successfully to other children who may come from different backgrounds, as this is what they will encounter in the larger world. Perhaps most of all, you want your children to believe in themselves and their self-worth such that they know they are capable of being successful in whatever they choose to do. They will need this sense of themselves as they take on more and more responsibility for their own choices and their future life and work.

Happy are those parents whose children look forward to going to school every day and become immersed in learning and in those things that most schools want them to learn. Some of the stated priorities from good schools include critical thinking, problem solving, self-expression, creativity and a continuing curiosity about the world and themselves. Many schools also emphasize the importance of being a compassionate, good citizen both in the school community and the larger neighborhood.

It's important to find a school and a program that fits the child and his or her needs. Instead of fitting the child to the school, think about fitting the school to the child. Too much of the "one size fits all" approach has resulted in students losing interest in learning, and they become bored, frustrated and disappointed with their school experiences. That is not a good formula for being happy or having a successful academic experience.

Here are three important considerations in choosing the right school:

1. The individual child and his or her needs and interests.
2. Parents' own expectations and values and how the school is or is not in accord with those.
3. Perhaps most importantly, the quality of the teachers and the culture of the school environment.

There is a process for evaluating each of these in some detail, and there is help available for parents who want to know more about how to select the most appropriate school for a child."[132]

Gary Gruber
Your Child, Your Choice: Finding the
Right School for Your Child

Parenting with Social and Emotional Learning: Thinking Before and After Actions

As parents, we want to be cognizant of the importance of helping our children grow socially and emotionally. Helping promote self-awareness, metacognition and reflection proves especially key in situations where young people make mistakes, which of course also leads to opportunities to grow. Read below for more on the importance of thinking before and after actions have been taken.

"Recently, after I witnessed a child hitting another child in the face on a playground, I heard his first words muttered through a steady stream of tears: 'I just wasn't thinking.' 'Think, think, think,' said Winnie the Pooh. And that silly old bear might have been wiser than Christopher Robin imagined. Stopping to think may not seem a priority in our fast-paced lives, but it just may be one key to raising socially- and emotionally-intelligent children. Sure there are <u>numerous ways</u> we can promote children's <u>self-awareness, self-management, social awareness, relationship skills and responsible decision-making</u>. We can model empathy just like the mother who regularly prepares meals for sick friends and whose child then replicated that lesson through her empathy for a friend who was in the hospital. We can coach our child when she is confused by a complexity of emotions by offering expressive language and asking, 'Is that the way you are feeling?' Or we can offer practice opportunities to help a child learn how to control his impulses. Instead of lashing out in anger, he'll later know how to express himself without harming others.

But we know time is limited, and parents become consumed by personal, social and career-related responsibilities. So you might ask, 'Is there just one practical way to focus my efforts to promote my child's success for today *and* for the future?' The answer: Yes, stop and think before and after acting. Planning and reflecting on experiences are central to any person's learning process. Our children see empathy in action. They think about it. They try it. They may reflect on it. Perhaps they improve how they respond, and the cycle continues. If our definition of success includes our child's ability to make positive choices when we are not present to guide him, then we must help him adopt strategies that will support his deep learning. In other words, he does not merely mimic what he sees in other's actions, but he also develops an understanding of why it is important. This kind of internalization of a skill only comes through observing, planning, trying it for oneself and reflecting. And fortunately, adding a thinking component to your life experiences can be simple as well as rewarding and enriching. Here are a few examples.

Practice thinking before acting. Model by thinking aloud. 'I want to go on a bike ride. What do I need to wear in order to prepare to stay safe during my ride? Hmmm ... I can put on my gym shoes and my helmet.' Instead of making quick decisions, guide your child with multiple small practice opportunities to stop and think before acting.

Set positive goals. Make a habit of talking about your child's hopes and how they can play out through his actions. 'You've been talking a lot about Evan. Do you hope to develop a friendship with him? Let's take the first step and invite him over for a play date.' Assist your child in articulating his desires in the form of a goal, and then talk about what small first step he can take toward that aim.

Predict consequences. When you stop and think with your child, ask her to predict the consequences of her actions. 'If you choose to jump from the top step to the bottom, what could happen?' or 'If you take that toy away from your sister, how do you think she'll react?' These small stop-and-think moments before taking action will help develop a critical habit that can pay off with bigger choices down the road.

Ask open-ended questions. So often, we play director as parents and, certainly, when safety is at stake; it's important that we do. But look for chances to ask questions that have no correct answer. Leave space for your child to think. Don't judge the response, but allow for creativity. 'What do you hope will happen?' or 'What choices do you have in this moment?' you might ask. You will promote problem-solving skills that will prove useful in a variety of contexts.

Reflect on thoughts and feelings with your child. In large part, children learn to define what they are feeling through your reactions and reflections. Use feeling language. So often, when people ask us how we are feeling, we share a thought instead. 'I feel like I could stand a break.' The thought is, 'I need a break.' The emotion, however, is, 'I feel tired and overwhelmed.' When you offer feeling language to interpret your child's expressions, ask if you are correct, or if she can help you better understand. Also, ask about others. 'How do you think Dad is feeling tonight?' prompting your son to try and take his dad's perspective and engage in empathic thinking.

Cultivate consequential thinking. Prompt thinking about cause and effect. 'Since you chose not to do your homework, what do you think the consequences are going to be for you?' Push yourself and your child to think of more than one result. In order to prepare children for that inevitable day in which they must choose between a decision that would make you proud or one that would disappoint you, they need plenty of practice thinking through the logical consequences of differing actions.

The ability to stop and think before acting—and reflecting in retrospect on choices made—can serve as critical tools in preparing children to be responsible decision-makers. What if each time a child has an impulse, he asks himself, 'What are possible actions that won't cause harm?' A child given support from a thoughtful family will develop the skills necessary to meet challenges in life with a considered approach. Start by asking yourself fundamental questions. Who do you want to be as a parent? What are your hopes for your children? What small daily actions align with those values and aspirations? Those deeply personal reflections will lead the way."[133]

Jennifer Miller
Parenting with Social and Emotional Learning:
Thinking Before and After Actions

Six Steps to Motivate Your Child

If you have ever been unmotivated to learn something, what spun it around for you? Following these steps can help turn an unmotivated student into one who is eager, curious and ready to engage and learn. Ready, set, go!

"How we make sense of learning is similar to how we make sense of other things. We do it gradually through experiences and building knowledge as we go. It's important to talk, think and reflect about learning. Just imagine your child—motivated and engaged while sharing what they learned and what they feel passionate about.

Use the following six strategies with your children:

1. Create a safe, flexible learning environment in which they can try new strategies and tools with multiple options to sit, stand, lie down and even pace. Find out if they need a quiet space to learn or whether they work better with music or noise in the background.

2. Review what teachers expect them to learn at school. Then ask them how they prefer or need to access information about the topic so that it makes sense to them. Encourage them to talk about different ways they like to obtain information. You may find they like to look up the information by themselves, watch a video or talk to you about it.

3. Talk about what they are learning and discuss if it is relevant to them and the real world. Some children have trouble with abstract ideas and need a personal connection so that it makes sense to them.

4. Make sure your child knows how to be safe and responsible online so he can be an effective global digital citizen.

5. Find out how your child likes and needs to engage with the content. You may find your child prefers to be outside, so help him do projects involving nature. Or if he enjoys working with another child, set up times for planning, working and playing.

6. Encourage children to reflect on their learning as they go. Reflection is personal, so invite your child to record thoughts in a journal. When they reflect and write, they will have to notice and think about their learning process. Some questions for them to consider as they write their reflection: What did I learn? How did I learn? What did I like? What would I do differently next time?"[134]

Barbara Bray
Learning is Personal for Your Child

10 Ways to Inspire a Love of Learning

Here are 10 recommendations for being intentional about inspiring lifelong learners, based on experiences from Carri's family.

1. **"Use a rainy or snowy day to learn something totally new together.** One snow day, my daughter and I tried <u>Hour of Code</u>, and I was amazed by how much she learned about coding and how much I learned about her.

2. **Launch an experiment that brings learning to life.** An afternoon getting inspired by an online '<u>Stick Bomb Tutorial</u>' taught us more about kinetic energy than we could ever learn in a textbook. It was so cool that the kids insisted we make some videos and share them with their friends. We uploaded the videos to Instagram and Facebook, and the kids were so excited to learn that they had inspired other friends to build their own stick bombs at home!

3. **Get out and explore.** There's definitely benefit to roaming around the woods without an agenda, but that doesn't mean learning can't happen there, too. Just last week, a bike ride turned into some impromptu trailblazing through a community nature preserve. We pointed out signs of changing seasons, compared natural and man-made things along the trail, identified fungus on logs, talked about compost and more. That 20-minute hike yielded a solid week's worth of science lessons.

4. **Take on personal challenges (and talk about overcoming them).** We're intentional about discussing how brains learn, and even our 4-year-old can describe how challenging a brain to process something new can help it 'grow.' We talk a lot about the importance of taking on mental and personal challenges, and we spend time reflecting on how that experience felt and how it improved us. It's important that inspiration flows both ways. So, for example, I recently shared with our 7-year-old how watching her swim and push herself to beat an end-of-the-season personal best time in butterfly inspired me to push myself to beat *my* personal best mile sprint time on the spinning bike.

5. **Turn something passive into something active.** Not every second of every day has to be tied to a specific learning goal, but there are times when parents can get creative to turn something passive into an active learning opportunity. Our youngest daughter is fascinated by toy review videos featuring other kids on YouTube. We'd rather her not spend too much time passively watching these videos, so instead I asked, 'Wouldn't you rather learn how to make your own video?' And, voila! We encouraged the kids to set up their own 'TV set,' make their own versions of the expensive toys on the YouTube channels and film their own reviews. Then we used iMovie to make a video and publish it online.

6. **Seek answers together.** We have a rule around here dictating that questions get answered to the best of our ability. 'Just because' and 'I don't know' are off the table. Instead, if one of the kids has a question

or one us is curious about something, we'll find the answer together. This works well for a few reasons. It teaches kids to follow their intellectual curiosities and to process that their interests have value, while at the same time giving them authentic research practice. Although the library can be a great way to spend an afternoon, not everything has to be a full-on study project. In our family, it's sometimes as simple as using Google to find the origin of the phrase 'getting a Charlie horse' or discovering all the ingredients in a McDonald's Shamrock Shake.

7. **Join (or start) a family book club.** Since my oldest daughter entered kindergarten, we've been in a monthly mother-daughter book club. Each month the hosting family rotates. When it's our turn, we choose the book for everyone to read, then lead the book talk, present a craft or activity, facilitate a potluck dinner and spend time together. Our club focuses on books that have strong female characters, but book clubs can be built around any theme or goal. During one of my favorite gatherings, we read 'The Evolution of Calpurnia Tate,' and, in the spirit of the main character, shared information about female scientists with our daughters. We then set up our own naturalist club for the afternoon—placing backyard discoveries under the microscope and adding them to our nature journals.

8. **Cultivate an interest in the arts.** Research supports the value found in exposing children to the arts, and doing so doesn't have to be expensive. We try to expose our kids to diverse experiences from bluegrass to ballet and from the contemporary arts to the classics. Seek out opportunities for free community concerts and family nights at local

museums. We've also been pleasantly surprised by the number of options available on services like Amazon Instant Video and Netflix to watch recorded videos of plays, concerts and shows like Cirque du Soleil.

9. **Stop and smell the roses.** Reflection is an important part of learning, so we try to create opportunities for our kids to slow down, practice mindfulness and reflect on the world around them. We like to collect treasures on neighborhood walks and to make nature mandalas when we get home.

10. **Everything is an opportunity to learn.** Parents, keep having fun with your kids, and don't be afraid to tell them they're learning along the way. Teach them that learning is fun, motivating and rewarding. Go rock climbing, and talk about pulleys. Set up a zip line, and talk about gravity and friction. Spray boiling water out of your kitchen window during a polar vortex, and talk about phase changes. Double a recipe. Pick berries. Write a letter. Walk across a frozen pond. Dig for worms. Find out how hot air balloons work. Go to the zoo. Plant an apple tree. Take a family art class. Climb a mountain. Build a birdhouse. Just keep learning."[135]

Carri Schneider
10 Ways to Inspire a Love of Learning

Parent Advocacy Strategies

We know parents are our children's first advocates. As parent Nancy Weinstein writes, advocacy in education can look different depending on the age and situation of the child. Here are some strategies to help parents advocate for their children.

"Step 1: Listen to your child

Start off knowing that no child wants to be unhappy, spend excessive time on homework or receive bad grades. Do your best to ask open-ended questions, and then sit back and listen. Once your child understands that you want to help and not criticize, the floodgates will open. The best time to do this, in my experience, is around bedtime. Snuggle up (if they will still let you), and ask them how their day was. Start by discussing who they sat with at lunch or who they partnered with in PE. The truth will come once they feel safe, knowing you won't blame or criticize.

Step 2: Talk to the teacher

Teachers want to help. Teachers can provide valuable insight your child can't provide. But they need to know you're not there to blame them. The teacher may notice a social dynamic your child won't share or observe another subtle yet consistent problem. Or they can help you investigate—pull out old tests, review last year's reports, find persisting patterns, etc. They have critical data you need.

If you're lucky, your search ends here. You can work with the teacher to address the problem directly. If it's a social issue, work with the teacher, the school counselor, the principal or the parent of the child who may be involved. If it's an academic problem, sometimes all you need is some extra support. Keep in mind that most academic subjects are cumulative, so you probably don't want to just 'wait it out.'

Step 3: Keep going

Even if the teacher says everything's fine, you can't stop here. Remember, you're the Chief Advocate. You know in your heart if your child's not fine. Parents are the ones who first identify 70 percent of learning problems. If you've reached this point, the problem likely won't fix itself without your help."[136]

Nancy Weinstein
Parents as Chief Advocates

10 Lessons for Learning and Life

Lessons for parents and teachers abound in this list from Mary Ryerse, including the importance of teaching perspective and empathy plus encouraging students to develop a vision.

1. **"Know your target.** Whether aiming for a bullseye in archery, a service box in tennis or a high note while singing, kids are accustomed to the concept of a target. In school, when students know outcomes toward which they are working (both learning goals and personal long-term goals), performance improves. Parents can help kids focus on simple targets like mastering a spelling list or more complex ones such as following a thesis statement or keeping life goals in mind.

2. **Keep it simple.** The more complex a repetitive motion, process or set of instructions is, the more room there is for error. Parents can help kids understand the big ideas, draw connections, be clear and not overcomplicate things. Thinking can be deep without being complex.

3. **Be consistent.** Easily one of the most important, but often overlooked hallmarks of good students is consistency. Regular study habits, attendance patterns, homework routines and attitudes all contribute to positive patterns of behavior that will equip young people for life responsibilities that lie ahead.

4. **Give full effort.** Encourage students to stay focused on what they can control (study habits, effort) rather than what they can't control.

5. **Use a common language.** One of understanding, patience, love and a huge smile. Kids living in a diverse world may not always speak the same language—literally and figuratively— as their classmates, their teachers or even family members. Some approaches transcend barriers. When we encourage students to greet classmates and teachers with a smile and a name, while presuming positive intent, everyone's learning environment improves.

6. **Lifting one person up could make everyone around you fly.** Including yourself. It is easy for students to see the competitive part of school. What if we also reinforced the act of helping others?

7. **Never, never, never give up.** This powerful lesson applies to doing a homework assignment, competing in an event or aiming to make good choices amidst an unfriendly middle school environment.

8. **Look at your abundance.** Help students see and be thankful for all the resources within them and around them. The list is infinite, but help them not to overlook their ability to learn, the teachers that can and will help them (especially if they ask!) and how their lives fit together as a whole.

9. **Make time for what's important.** This helps students prioritize work, but don't forget to take care of yourself and your family. Put first things first.

10. Live in a way that you'll want to do it all over again. Not because you need a 'do-over,' but because you feel so good about what you did.

Underlying the capacity to deliver the above lessons is a foundational practice that applies especially to parents and teachers: seeing with 'double vision.' Simply stated, as parents, we can unleash potential when we simultaneously see our kids as they are now and as they can be (hence the double vision)."[137]

Mary Ryerse
Lessons for Learning and Life: 10 Messages Parents (and Teachers) Can Teach Kids

Helping Students Define Success

Parents who help their children define success for themselves encourage and challenge their students, allowing them to learn on their own terms. Here, Ryan Makhani brings up 10 ways parents can help children define what success means.

1. "The parents are aware of their own fears and dreams.
2. The parents encourage and challenge their children rather than control all their decisions.
3. The parents do not impose their definition of success on their children; instead, they have conversations to help guide what success could mean and what it could look like for their child.
4. The parents ask questions that encourage children to find their own passions and define their goals.
5. The parents provide tools for the child to explore and to imagine their possibilities.
6. The parents help the child not compare themselves to others, but rather to focus on their own growth.
7. The parents support the child's curiosity and listen in ways that the child feels supported.
8. The parents take time to know their children in regard to what pushes their buttons, what motivates them and what they love.
9. The parents encourage the child's play in areas that could become a lifelong passion.
10. The parents recognize that the context in which their child is growing up differs significantly from their own childhood."[138]

Ryan Makhani
Parents, Help Your Child Define Success For Themselves

10 Principles to Inspire a Love of Learning in Nature

Kids benefit from learning outside, and the good news is, according to PBS Kids' Dr. Scott Sampson, there are plenty of opportunities exist to encourage just that right outside your window. As the old saying goes, there's no such thing as bad weather—just bad clothing. So get outside, and get playing!

1. **"Make new habits.** Take some time to discover the varieties of nature close to your home, and explore these places with your children. Most young children will have no problem engaging with their natural surroundings. Their curious minds are built to do just that. Older children who've established a preference for electronic screens may take a little more coaxing; this is where grown-ups need to exercise some imagination and perhaps even foster a trickster mentality. Rather than telling children they need to go out because it's good for them, think about encouraging them to play games like tag and 'Kick the Can.' The key here is to establish nature as the fun and preferred option for playtime.

2. **Open senses and expand awarenes.** Play around with having 'deer ears' and 'owl eyes.' Deer have amazing hearing, thanks in part to their very large ears, which capture even the faintest of sounds. Try having children cup their hands behind their ears to listen carefully. Ask them to detect the most distant sound they can hear and to identify the total number of different noises they detect. Similarly, owls have

amazing eyesight. Invite kids to soften their vision so that they can see as much as possible in all different directions. What is the most distant thing they can see? On subsequent visits outdoors, pause once in a while to remind kids to use their 'deer ears' and 'owl eyes.'

3. **Free play rules!** Carve out some regular time for the children in your life to engage in unstructured play, a portion of it taking place outdoors. 'Unstructured' refers to free play without adult guidance or supervision. Encourage kids to create their own imaginative games and activities, preferably using readily available natural elements like water, sticks, dirt and rocks.

4. **Start sit spotting.** Find a place in a natural setting where you can sit and observe. Pick a place that's nearby—for example, in the backyard, courtyard or neighborhood park—so that it's easy to get to. Visit your sit spot regularly, preferably daily or at least several times a week; sit quietly there, observing with all your senses. Vary the time of day you go, enjoying morning, noon and nighttime sights to see how your sit spot changes. Eventually, you will know this little corner of the universe better than anyone else. You'll quickly find that this activity changes the way you and the youngsters experience your home and immediate surroundings.

5. **Become a hummingbird parent.** Instead of helicopter parenting, work on developing your flight skills as a hummingbird parent. This means giving kids enough space and autonomy to take risks, staying on the periphery sipping nectar most of the time and zooming in only when necessary.

6. **Questioning.** After kids spend time outdoors, ask them what happened. What did they see, hear and feel? What was their favorite story of the day? Make sure the bulk of your questions are easy to answer, particularly at the start, so as to build confidence. Once in a while, drop in a challenging question—something you may not have the answer to that rests just beyond the kids' edges. Then return to that mystery once in a while to see if they've made any progress. In addition to the lessons learned, asking questions shows that you value both nature and the children's experience.

7. **Venture into the bubble.** An essential ingredient of nature connection involves learning to see animals, plants and other life forms as subjects rather than objects. One method is the 'soap bubble technique,' invented by German biologist Jakob von Uexküll. Head outside, and picture every plant and animal surrounded by a soap bubble that represents its own individual sensory world. Now imagine being able to step inside the bubble of your choice—say, of a robin, earthworm, butterfly or pine tree. Encourage kids to find their favorite animal, enter the imaginary bubble and experience this alternate world. You might ask questions like, 'Do slugs see?' and 'Why do you think that bird is singing?' Ideally, these questions will lead to unknown answers that inspire more curiosity. Of course, the soap bubble technique can be aided by some knowledge of the sensory world of the creature in question, but such understanding isn't necessary. It's the imagination stoked that counts the most.

8. **Nature connection is a contact sport.** Too often these days, children's encounters with nature become dominated by a look-but-don't-touch directive. Na-

ture connections depend on firsthand, multisensory encounters. It's a messy, dirty business —picking leaves and flowers, turning over rocks, holding wriggling worms, splashing in ponds. Rather than telling kids 'no' all the time when they want to climb a tree, throw a rock or step into a muddy pond, take a deep breath and offer words of encouragement. Don't worry so much about the dirt and scrapes. Clothes and bodies can be washed, and cuts heal.

9. **Snap some nature photos.** Screens have become a major part of our lives. So think about ways to use digital technologies to leverage a nature connection. For example, encourage kids to take a camera outside and take photos of five natural things that interest them—flowers, bugs, rocks, whatever. Then invite them to open their senses and spend at least five minutes closely observing their surroundings, including tiny things like ants and giant things like clouds. Afterward, feel free to encourage the electronic sharing of any products, an easy avenue to blend the digital and natural worlds.

10. **Discover your own nature- passion.** If you haven't yet found a nature activity that you're passionate about, think about it. Yes, most of us are extremely busy and find it difficult to carve out time for anything new. But the reality is that most young kids these days aren't going to get out into nature unless we take them there. So try to find an activity—whether it's close to home, like gardening, or far away, like fly fishing or snowshoeing— that you can engage in with the children in your life."[139]

Dr. Scott Sampson
How to Raise A Wild Child: The Art and
Science of Falling in Love with Nature

Appendices

Appendix A: About the Authors

Appendix B: Contributor Bios and Posts

Appendix C: Glossary

Appendix D: Disclosures

Appendix A: About the Authors

Bonnie Lathram is Learner Experience Manager and Contributing Author at Getting Smart. She has taught elementary, middle and high school students in the United States and Tanzania. She honed her skills working with students, mentors and families at an innovative public high school near Seattle. She has also led professional development for school-based teams in the U.S. and abroad. Bonnie has also co-authored several publications including Big Picture Learning's guide on metacognitive factors related to student success in colleges and careers. She has a Master's Degree in Education and lives with her husband Ryan and two children in Seattle.

Carri Schneider is Director of Knowledge Design at Getting Smart. She has taught in classrooms from elementary schools to college campuses and online. She is co-author of the books "Navigating the Digital Shift" and "Building a 21st Century U.S. Education System," and has written extensively on the future of education. She holds an M.Ed. in educational administration and an Ed.D. in urban educational leadership, with an emphasis on education and social justice. Carri and her husband Lou live in Cincinnati with their two school-aged daughters.

Tom Vander Ark is author of "Getting Smart: How Digital Learning is Changing the World" and "Smart Cities That Work for Everyone: 7 Keys to Education & Employment." He is CEO of Getting Smart, a learning design firm and a partner at Learn Capital, an education venture fund. Previously, he served as the first Executive Director of Education for the Bill & Melinda Gates Foundation. Tom served as a public school superintendent in Washington state and has extensive private sector experience. Tom is Director for the International Association for K-12 Online Learning (iNACOL), Imagination Foundation and Charter Board Partners. Tom and his wife Karen have two grown daughters.

Appendix B: Contributor Bios and Posts

All authors listed contributed to our Smart Parents blog series. The series can be found on GettingSmart.com and The Huffington Post.

Curt Allen is CEO of Agilix.
Blog Post: Learning Gets Personal: What Personalized Learning Means to the Allen Family

Lara Allen studied piano performance at BYU and BU and is head of fine arts at her children's school.
Blog Post: Learning Gets Personal: What Personalized Learning Means to the Allen Family

Jose Arenas leads Innovate Public Schools' parent organizing team.
Blog Post: Organized Parents Can Transform Education. Indeed, It Won't Happen Without Them

Carol Barash, Ph.D., is founder and CEO of Story2 and author of "Write Out Loud."
Blog Post: 10 Things Parents of High School Juniors Should Start Doing Now

Heather Benedict lives in the suburbs of Charlotte, NC, with her husband and their 7-year-old daughter Aislinn.
Blog Post: Why We Need to Teach Students to be Self-Advocates

Alfred Binford is managing director of Assessment and Direct Delivery for Pearson North America.
Blog Post: Today's Busy Families Are Finding Time to Gather Around the Dinner Table

Marie Bjerede is a #mathmom, #makermom, recovering telecom executive and citizen advocate for education as a platform.
Blog Post: What Personalized Learning Means in My Family

Arina Bokas, Ph.D., is Clarkston PTA Council president at Clarkston Community Schools, a host of the public TV series "The Future of Learning" and on the faculty of Mott Community College in Michigan.
Blog Post: Changing the Mindset of Education: Every Learner is Unique

Barbara Bray is co-founder of Personalize Learning, LLC.
Blog Post: Learning is Personal for Your Child

Eduardo Briceño is the co-founder and CEO of Mindset Works.
Blog Post: Growth Mindset Parenting

Mira Browne is chief external officer of Summit Public Schools.
Blog Post: Graduating Self-Directed Learners Ready To Thrive in College

Dr. Alison Bryant is co-CEO and chief play officer at Play Science.
Blog Post: Lessons for Parents on Pink Versus Blue Tech

Christine Byrd is communications manager for the education nonprofit MIND Research Institute.
Blog Post: 8 Ways Blended Learning Changes the Game

Betty Chen is director of family engagement at Summit Public Schools.
Blog Post: Graduating Self-Directed Learners Ready to Thrive in College

Tracy Clark is a former bilingual teacher-turned-teacher educator, writer and co-organizer for EdTechWomen Austin.
Blog Post: To My Son's Future Teacher

Karen Copeland is the parent of two children and lives in Abbotsford, British Columbia. She writes on her website Champions for Community Mental Wellness about her journey as a parent of a child who experiences mental health challenges.
Blog Post: I Am "That" Parent

Susan Lucille Davis teaches 7th- and 8th-grade English at the 'Iolani School in Honolulu, Hawaii.
Blog Post: 10 Reasons Why I Want My Students to Blog

Nicholas C. Donohue is president and CEO of the Nellie Mae Education Foundation.
Blog Post: Why Student-Centered Learning Matters

Debra Dye is the mother of three children, including two who have been diagnosed with dyslexia.
Blog Post: Mississippi Mother: I Was Not Going to Let My Sons Become Yet Another Tragic Statistic

Joe Eames is a consultant and freelance trainer for Pluralsight.com.
Blog Post: The 16-Year-Old Coder: Why My Daughter No Longer Attends Public High School

Richard Ferguson is a "higher education innovator" and former CEO and founder of ACT.
Blog Post: Sage Advice From a Higher Ed Veteran: Getting a Head Start on Finding the Right College

Jamey Fitzpatrick is the president and CEO of Michigan Virtual University.
Blog Post: <u>Leveraging Innovative Policy Options for Students</u>

Alyssa Frank is managing editor at Roadtrip Nation.
Blog Post: <u>Doctor, Lawyer, Camel Rancher? Helping Your Kids Discover Careers They Love</u>

Lisa Guernsey is director of the Learning Technologies Project and director of the Early Education Initiative in New America's Education Policy Program.
Blog Post: <u>Common Sense, Science-Based Advice on Early Learners' Screen Time</u>

Gary Gruber is a lifelong learner, educator and consultant to schools in transition.
Blog Post: <u>Your Child, Your Choice: Choosing a School for Your Child</u>

Michael Harlow is a consultant in education and workforce policy, serving on the Northwest Local Board of Education.
Blog Post: <u>If Ever There Was a Kid Born to Read</u>

Grant Hosford is CEO of codeSpark.
Blog Post: <u>Do Your Kids Need to Learn to Code? YES! But Not for the Reasons You Think</u>

Carol Iles is the mother of three children, including 6-year-old Kasey with special needs.
Blog Post: <u>Don't Let a Piece of Paper Put Children in an Educational Box</u>

Bill Jackson is the founder of GreatSchools.
Blog Post: <u>Parental Perfection, Reimagined</u>

Frances Jensen, M.D. is chair of the Department of Neurology at the Perelman School of Medicine, University of Pennsylvania, and author of the New York Times bestseller, "The Teenage Brain: A Neuroscientist's Survival Guide to Raising Adolescents and Young Adults."
Blog Post: The Teenage Brain: Scaffolding the Brain for Lifelong Learning

Jenna Kleine is ClassDojo's community lead.
Blog Post: Family, Teacher Comms 101: 4 Simple Ways to Build Better Relationships with Your Child's Teachers

Ryan Makhani is the founder of BuildMyIdea.org.
Blog Post: 10 Strategies to Help Children Define Success for Themselves

Duncan McCrann is the chief administrative officer at Educational Enterprises.
Blog Post: The Power of Parents, Teachers and Technology in Character Education

Megan Mead is growth services manager and math contributor at Getting Smart.
Blog Post: Understanding Your Middle Schooler: 4 Tips for Success

Jennifer Miller is author and illustrator of the blog Confident Parents Confident Kids and an expert contributor to NBC Universal's Parent Toolkit.
Blog Post: The Power of Parenting with Social and Emotional Learning, Parenting with Social and Emotional Learning: Thinking Before and After Actions

Michelle Miller is managing director of the Joan Ganz Cooney Center and mom to a toddler being raised in NYC.

Blog Post: How to Turn Screen Time into Family Time

Kris Perry is the executive director of the First Five Years Fund.
Blog Post: Early Childhood Education is Critical for Our Own Kids' Future—And the Nation's

Karla Phillips is a policy director at the Foundation for Excellence in Education.
Blog Posts: Vanessa's Journey: Empowering Special Education Through Technology, A Choosy Mom on Choosing Schools, When Diplomas and Credits Send False Signals

Katherine Prince is a senior director at Strategic Foresight at KnowledgeWorks.
Blog Post: I Need a Learning Sherpa

Beth Purcell is president of PublicSchoolOptions.org.
Blog Post: Trust Parents with Educational Choice

Nina Rees is the president and CEO of the National Alliance for Public Charter Schools.
Blog Post: 3 Factors to Consider When Choosing an Innovative School

Patrick Riccards is the chief communications and strategy officer for the Woodrow Wilson Foundation and author of the award-winning Dadprovement book.
Blog Post: What Relationships Drive Learning? Try Fathers

Rod Rock, Ed.D., is superintendent of Clarkston Community Schools.
Blog Post: Changing the Mindset of Education: Every Learner is Unique

Mary Ryerse is director of strategic design at Getting Smart and co-author of numerous publications and books including "Smart Cities That Work for Everyone: 7 Keys to Education & Employment."
Blog Posts: Beyond Information: Engaging Parents (and Students) in Choosing Great Schools, Add to the School Supply List: Mindsets Emphasizing Effort, Attitude, and Respect, You Can Thank Mom for More Than the Meal Itself: Family Dinner Matters and Lessons for Learning and Life: 10 Messages Parents (and Teachers) Can Teach Kids

Dr. Scott Sampson is a dinosaur paleontologist and science communicator who hosts the PBS KIDS television series "Dinosaur Train."
Blog Post: How to Raise a Wild Child: The Art and Science of Falling in Love with Nature

Angela Shelton-Garofano is a mom of two, including an ASD son, and an independent senior director at Thirty-One Gifts.
Blog Post: Why Online Learning Works for My Family

Max Silverman is associate director at the University of Washington Center for Educational Leadership.
Blog Post: One Family's Journey Exemplifies Anytime-Anywhere Learning

Antonia Slagle is a mom of three boys and an elementary principal in Isleton, California.
Blog Post: Ready for the World: Redefining Success in the Age of Change

Jessica Slusser is project coordinator at Getting Smart.
Blog Post: Why Online Learning Works for Parents and Kids

Heather Staker is the president and founder of <u>Ready to Blend</u>, as well as an adjunct researcher for the Christensen Institute.
Blog Post: <u>How to Keep Children from Drowning in the Device Deep End and Why An Anti-Screen Family Has Gone Blended</u>

Solomon Steplight is founder of Prepfoleo.
Blog Post: <u>How Parents Decide Which Education Materials Work</u>

Jason Stirman is a product designer at Medium.
Blog Post: <u>I Received This Email from My Son's Principal</u>

Cara Thorpe, M.Ed., is the founder and president of <u>K-12 Learning Solutions</u>.
Blog Post: <u>The Power of Personal Relationship in Personalized Learning</u>

Caroline Vander Ark is COO at Getting Smart.
Blog Post: <u>Why I Hate Pink: Abandoning Gender Stereotypes</u>

Sarah Maraniss Vander Schaaff is a writer and the managing editor for media and content for <u>Mindprint Learning</u>.
Blog Posts: <u>Never the First to Finish: Why Pace Matters</u> and <u>Why Mentors Matter</u>

Katrina Waidelich is a curriculum writer at RoadTrip Nation.
Blog Post: <u>Doctor, Lawyer, Camel Rancher? Helping Your Kids Discover Careers They Love</u>

Tatyana Warrick is director of communications for Partnership for 21st-Century Learning.

Blog Post: <u>5 Ways Parents Can Encourage 21st-Century Learning</u>

Nancy Weinstein is the founder and CEO of <u>Mindprint Learning</u>.
Blog Post: <u>Parents as Chief Advocates</u>

John Weiss is Director of Strategic Initiatives at the Neutral Zone, Ann Arbor Teen Center.
Blog Post: <u>Why Letting Youth Run the Store Is Important for their Development and Life Success</u>

Sue Wilkes provides capacity-building support and training for nonprofit organizations in the Puget Sound area.
Blog Post: <u>One Family's Journey Exemplifies Anytime-Anywhere Learning</u>

Liz Wimmer is a writer with the National Center on Quality Teaching and Learning at the University of Washington.
Blog Posts: <u>What Do Parents Want from Schools? Hint: Think Car Shopping</u>, <u>As the World Changes, So Must Education</u>, <u>The Elementary Years: Four Pillars That Build a Strong Foundation</u>

Janice Wyatt-Ross, Ed.D., is an assistant professor in the School of Education at Asbury University and mother of two teenage daughters.
Blog Post: <u>Kids, Smart Phones and Social Media: 6 Rules for Success and Safety</u>

Greg Young is an educator and administrator with the Virtual Learning Academy in New Hampshire and a school design coach with Big Picture Learning.
Blog Post: <u>Power of Play: Applied Knowledge, Engaged Learning</u>

Appendix C: Glossary

21st-Century Skills are those that students will need for life and work in an increasingly complex era. These include communication, collaboration, flexibility, problem solving, creativity, global literacy and technology.

Blended Learning is a mix of online and in-person learning opportunities that combine to make a cohesive educational program.

Competency-Based Learning means that students can advance when they demonstrate competency in measurable learning objectives.

Deeper Learning requires students to be actively engaged in their learning—seeking new information and applying it in meaningful ways.

Flipped Learning describes when individuals receive direct instruction, then gather as a group with a guide or teacher to discuss concepts, solve problems and apply knowledge.

Performance-Based Assessments allow students to demonstrate their knowledge and skills and to show how they solved problems.

Personalized Learning is learning that is responsive to the needs of each student. Teachers can provide personalized learning by offering a variety of ways to learn skills and by helping students create unique learning plans.

Project-Based Learning is a teaching method where students learn by working for an extended period of time, responding to a complex question, problem or challenge.

Online Learning refers to Internet-based learning opportunities.

Online Schools deliver education on the Web.

Student-Led Conferences are parent-teacher conferences that students attend and lead.

Student-Led Exhibitions are presentations of student work, led by students.

Student-Centered Learning is a model in which students take responsibility for their learning, help create and follow an individualized learning plan, and demonstrate their skills and knowledge. Students also have the freedom to learn in a variety of settings and at times that work best for them.

Appendix D: Disclosures

The authors have a relationship with some of the organizations mentioned as shown below.

Getting Smart Advocacy Partners
Agilix
Connections Education
DreamBox Learning
The Bill & Melinda Gates Foundation
Innovate Public Schools
MIND Research Institute
PresenceLearning

Organization where Tom serves as a Director
Imagination Foundation

Learn Capital Portfolio Companies
Class Dojo
DIY.org
Udemy

Endnotes

1. Vander Ark, T. "Everything is Different Now: Parenting for Powerful Learning." Getting Smart blog. March 2015. http://gettingsmart.com/2015/03/everything-is-different-now-parenting-for-powerful-learning-2/

2. Vander Ark, T. "Push Learning: How Smart Notifications Will Change Education." Getting Smart blog. May 2015. http://gettingsmart.com/2015/05/push-learning-how-smart-notifications-will-change-education/

3. Staker, H. "Why an Anti-Screen Family Has Gone Blended." Getting Smart blog. August 2015. http://gettingsmart.com/2015/07/why-an-anti-screen-family-has-gone-blended/

4. Vander Ark, T. "Five Trends Demand Smart States." Getting Smart blog. June 2015. http://gettingsmart.com/2015/06/five-trends-demand-smart-states/

5. Vander Ark, T. "Why Cultivating Nonconformity is More Important Than Ever." Getting Smart blog. June 2015. http://gettingsmart.com/2015/06/why-cultivating-nonconformity-is-more-important-than-ever/

6. Big Picture Learning. The Role of Noncognitive Skills for Student Success. Big Picture Company. 2014. https://itunes.apple.com/us/book/role-noncognitive-skills-for/id904019800?mt=11

7. Prince, K. "I Need a Learning Sherpa." Getting Smart blog. February 2015. http://gettingsmart.com/2015/02/need-learning-sherpa/

8. Steplight, S. "How Parents Decide Which Education Materials Work." Getting Smart blog. May 2015. http://gettingsmart.com/2015/05/how-parents-decide-which-education-materials-work/

9. In Consultants Steer Parents Through a Maze of School Choice, this phenomenon is clear. "The rapid expansion of charter schools and other public school options is fueling growth in another industry: education consulting. Education consultants, once used primarily by families to help them select and get into elite private

schools, are now being hired by parents in New York City, Denver, and Washington to help them navigate a plethora of public school options."

10. Jackson, B. "Parental Perfection, Reimagined." Getting Smart blog. May 2015. http://gettingsmart.com/2015/05/parental-perfection-reimagined/

11. Ibid.

12. Hill, A. "Exclusive survey: Parents weigh in on the digital classroom." Marketplace Learning Curve. May 2015. http://www.marketplace.org/topics/education/learning-curve/exclusive-survey-parents-weigh-digital-classroom

13. Vander Ark, T. "Modeling Good Work." Getting Smart blog. May 2015. http://gettingsmart.com/2015/05/modeling-good-work/

14. Press Release. U.S. Secretary of Education Arne Duncan Announces a Set of Rights to Help Parents Seek High Quality Education for Their Children, June 26, 2015. http://www.ed.gov/news/press-releases/us-education-secretary-arne-duncan-announces-set-rights-help-parents-seek-high-quality-education-their-children

15. Adair, J. "The March jobs report is worse than we thought." Young Invincibles. April 2015. http://younginvincibles.org/tag/young-adult-unemployment/

16. Bidwell, A. "Average Student Loan Debt Approaches $30,000." U.S. News and Report. November 13, 2014. http://www.usnews.com/news/articles/2014/11/13/average-student-loan-debt-hits-30-000

17. Warrick, T. "5 Ways Parents Can Encourage 21st Century Learning." Getting Smart blog. May 2015. http://gettingsmart.com/2015/05/5-ways-parents-can-encourage-21st-century-learning/

18. Vander Ark, T. "Most Likely to Succeed: A Film About What School Could Be." Getting Smart blog. March 2015. http://gettingsmart.com/2015/03/likely-succeed-film-school/

19. Rees, N. "3 Factors to Consider When Choosing an Innovative School." Getting Smart blog. March 2015. http://gettingsmart.com/2015/03/3-factors-to-consider-when-choosing-an-innovative-school/

20. Levine, M. "Five Things I've Learned." Thefivethings.org. http://www.thefivethings.org/michael-levine/#

21. Briceño, E. "Growth Mindset Parenting." Getting Smart blog. May 2015. http://gettingsmart.com/2015/03/growth-mindset-parenting/

22. Bronson, P. "How Not to Talk to Your Kids." New York Magazine. August 3, 2007. http://nymag.com/news/features/27840

23. Bokas, A. and Rock, R. "Changing the Mindset of Education: Every Learner is Unique." Getting Smart blog. May 2015. http://gettingsmart.com/2015/05/changing-the-mindset-of-education-every-learner-is-unique/

24. Nagaoka, J., Farrington, C., Ehrlich, S. and Heath, R. with Johnson, D., Dickson, S., Turner, A.C., Mayo, A. and Hayes, K. "Foundations for Young Adult Success A Developmental Framework." June 2015. The University of Chicago CCSR. https://ccsr.uchicago.edu/publications/foundations-young-adult-success-developmental-framework

25. CASEL. "Social and Emotional Learning Core Competencies." http://www.casel.org/social-and-emotional-learning/core-competencies

26. http://www.epiconline.org

27. "What is Deeper Learning?" The William and Flora Hewlett Foundation. http://www.hewlett.org/programs/education/deeper-learning/what-deeper-learning

28. Warrick, T. "5 Ways Parents Can Encourage 21st Century Learning." Getting Smart blog. May 2015. http://gettingsmart.com/2015/05/5-ways-parents-can-encourage-21st-century-learning/

29. "The Science: The Growth Mindset." Mindset Works. http://www.mindsetworks.com/webnav/whatismindset.aspx

30. See info on William Sedlacek. http://www.williamsedlacek.info

31. Vander Ark, C. "Why I Hate Pink: Abandoning Gender Stereotypes." Getting Smart blog. April 2015. http://gettingsmart.com/2015/04/why-i-hate-pink-abandoning-gender-stereotypes/

32. Vander Ark, T. "The Learning Design Opportunity of Our Time." Getting Smart blog. October 2, 2012. http://gettingsmart.com/2012/10/the-learning-design-opportunity-our-time/

33. Browne, M. and Chen, B. "Graduating Self-Directed Learners Ready to Thrive in College." Getting Smart blog. May 2015. http://gettingsmart.com/2015/05/graduating-self-directed-learners-ready-to-thrive-in-college/

34. Briceño, E. "Growth Mindset Parenting." Getting Smart blog May 2015. http://gettingsmart.com/2015/03/growth-mindset-parenting/

35. Schneider, C. "Smart Parent Tip: See Inside Out." Getting Smart blog. June 2015. http://gettingsmart.com/2015/06/smart-parent-tip-see-inside-out/

36. Miller, J. "The Power of Parenting with Social and Emotional

Learning." Getting Smart blog. April 2015. http://gettingsmart.com/2015/04/the-power-of-parenting-with-social-and-emotional-learning/

37. Bjerede, M. "What Personalized Learning Means in My Family." Getting Smart blog. February 2015. http://gettingsmart.com/2015/02/personalized-learning-means-family/

38. Ryerse, M., Schneider, C. and Vander Ark, T. "Core & More: Guiding and Personalizing College & Career Readiness." Getting Smart. May 2014. http://gettingsmart.com/publication/core-guiding-personalizing-college-career-readiness/

39. Cushman, K. "8 Universal Secrets of Motivated Learners." Personalize Learning blog and webinar. November 2013. http://www.personalizelearning.com/2013/11/8-universal-secrets-of-motivated.html

40. Ryerse, M. "Music Builds Maker Mindsets: The Power of the Performing Arts." Getting Smart blog. March 2015. http://gettingsmart.com/2015/03/music-builds-maker-mindsets-the-power-of-the-performing-arts/

41. Vander Ark, T. "The Quest for an AA Degree in High School." Getting smart blog. January 2015. http://gettingsmart.com/2015/01/quest-aa-degree-high-school/

42. Weinstein, N. "Parents as Chief Advocates." Smart Parents blog. March 2015. http://gettingsmart.com/2015/03/parents-as-chief-advocates/

43. Copeland, K. "I Am 'That' Parent." Getting Smart blog. April 2015. http://gettingsmart.com/2015/04/i-am-that-parent/

44. Arenas, J. "Organized Parents Can Transform Education- Indeed, It Won't Happen Without Them." Getting Smart blog. August 2015. http://gettingsmart.com/2015/08organized-parents-can-transform-education-indeed-it-wont-happen-without-them/

45. Phillips, K. "A Choosy Mom on Choosing Schools." Getting Smart blog. May 2015. http://gettingsmart.com/2015/05/a-choosy-mom-on-choosing-schools/

46. Purcell, B. "Trust Parents With Educational Choice." Getting Smart blog. June 2015. http://gettingsmart.com/2015/06/trust-parents-with-educational-choice/

47. "What's the Best School for My Child?" Raising Special Kids. Spring 2015. http://www.raisingspecialkids.org/_media/uploaded/c/0e4190992_1430250027_connecting-spring-2015-final-web.pdf

48. Phillips, K. "A Choosy Mom on Choosing Schools." Getting

Smart blog. May 2015. http://gettingsmart.com/2015/05/a-choosy-mom-on-choosing-schools/

49. Allen, C. "Learning Gets Personal: What Personalized Learning Means to the Allen Family." Getting Smart blog. June 2015. http://gettingsmart.com/2015/06/learning-gets-personal-what-personalized-learning-means-to-the-allen-family/

50. Vander Schaaff, S. "Why Mentors Matter." Getting Smart blog. April 2015. http://gettingsmart.com/2015/04/why-mentors-matter/

51. Ryerse, M., Schneider, C. and Vander Ark, T. "Core and More: Guiding and Personalizing College & Career Readiness." Digital Learning Now. May 2014. http://digitallearningnow.com/site/uploads/2014/05/FINAL-Smart-Series-Core-and-More-Guidance.pdf

52. "Student-centered Schools: Closing the Opportunity Gap." Stanford Graduate School of Education. http://edpolicy.stanford.edu/projects/633

53. Lenz, B. "A Case for Student-Centered Learning." Edutopia blog. Februaray 2014. http://www.edutopia.org/blog/a-case-for-student-centered-learning-bob-lenz

54. Riccards, P. "What Relationships Drive Learning? Try Fathers." Getting Smart blog. March 2015. http://gettingsmart.com/2015/03/what-relationships-drive-learning-try-fathers/

55. Slagle, A. "Ready For The World: Redefining Success In The Age Of Change." Getting Smart blog. March 2015. http://gettingsmart.com/2015/03/ready-for-the-world-redefining-success-in-the-age-of-change/

56. Shelton-Garofano, A. "Why Online Learning Works for My Family." Getting Smart blog. August 2015. http://gettingsmart.com/2015/07/why-online-learning-works-for-my-family/

57. Nellie Mae Education Foundation. http://www.nmefoundation.org/our-vision/competency-based

58. "What is Competency Education?" http://www.competencyworks.org/about/competency-education/

59. Ibid.

60. Sturgis, C. "Doing it Yourself: From Independent Learning Plans to Organizing Your Instructional Path." Getting Smart blog. March 2015. http://gettingsmart.com/2015/03/independent-learning-plans-organizing-instructional-path/

61. Nellie Mae Education Foundation. http://www.nmefoundation.org/our-vision/competency-based

62.   Byrd, C. "8 Ways Blended Learning Changes the Game." Getting Smart blog. March 2015. http://gettingsmart.com/2015/03/8-ways-blended-makes-learning-fun-starting-in-kindergarten/

63.   Vander Schaaff, S. "Never The First to Finish: Why Pace Matters." Getting Smart blog. January 2015. http://gettingsmart.com/2015/01/never-first-finish-pace-matters/

64.   Phillips, K. "Vanessa's Journey: Empowering Special Education Through Technology." Getting Smart blog. April 2015. http://gettingsmart.com/2015/04/vanessas-journey-empowering-special-education-through-technology/

65.   Evergreen Education Group. "Keeping Pace with Digital Learning." 2014, 11th edition. http://www.kpk12.com/wp-content/uploads/EEG_KP2014-fnl-lr.pdf

66.   Schneider, C. "Advice for Analog Parents with Digital Kids." Getting Smart blog. June 2015. http://gettingsmart.com/2015/06/advice-for-analog-parents-with-digital-kids/

67.   http://digitallearningnow.com/report-card/#grade2

68.   Fitzpatrick, J. "Leveraging Innovative Policy Options for Students." Getting Smart blog. March 2015. http://gettingsmart.com/2015/03/leveraging-innovative-policy-options-for-students/

69.   Ibid.

70.   Ichinose, C. "A Teacher's Experience: What I Learned Working in Online Schools." Getting Smart blog. January 2014. http://gettingsmart.com/2014/01/teachers-experience-learned-working-online-schools/

71.   Digital Learning Now. "Blended Learning Implementation Guide." http://digitallearningnow.com/site/uploads/2013/10/BLIG-2.0-Final-Paper.pdf

72.   Mead, M. "Telehealth: The Next-Generation of Therapy." Getting Smart blog. September 2014. http://gettingsmart.com/2014/09/next-generation-online-therapy/

73.   See http://gettingsmart.com/publication/data-backpacks-portable-records-learner-profiles/ for more information.

74.   Find info on the number of apps available in leading app stores as of May 2015 at Statista. http://www.statista.com/statistics/276623/number-of-apps-available-in-leading-app-stores/

75.   Dobrow, J. "The App Gap: Debating and Rating 'Educational' Apps for Kids." The Huffington Post. February 2015. http://www.huffingtonpost.com/julie-dobrow/the-app-gap-debating-and-rating-educational-apps_b_6699290.html

76. Hernandez, A. "Toddlers and Tablets." Education Next. Winter 2014. http://educationnext.org/toddlers-and-tablets/

77. Davis, S.L. "10 Reasons Why I Want My Students to Blog." Getting Smart blog. October 2012. http://gettingsmart.com/2012/10/10-reasons-why-i-want-my-students-blog/

78. Anderson, A. "There's a Maker Faire in That iPad! 10 Ways to Create Student Makers With Apps." Getting Smart blog. February 2014. http://gettingsmart.com/2014/02/theres-maker-fair-pad-10-ways-create-student-makers-apps/

79. Mead, M. "blink blink Designs Educational Tech Kits with Girls, for Girls." Getting Smart blog. May 2015. http://gettingsmart.com/2015/05/blink-blink-designs-educational-tech-kits-with-girls-for-girls/

80. Hosford, G. "Do Your Kids Need to Learn to Code? YES! But Not for the Reasons You Think." Getting Smart blog. May 2015. http://gettingsmart.com/2015/05/do-your-kids-need-to-learn-to-code-yes-but-not-for-the-reasons-you-think/

81. Vander Ark, T. "Drop Everything and Sail the World." Getting Smart blog. June 2015. http://gettingsmart.com/2015/05/do-your-kids-need-to-learn-to-code-yes-but-not-for-the-reasons-you-think/

82. Conry, J. "The benefits of slow parenting." The Boston Globe. May 11, 2015. http://www.bostonglobe.com/lifestyle/2015/05/10/the-benefits-slow-parenting/2LImOAIyqElORCStgOADSI/story.html

83. Ibid.

84. Schneider, C. "10 Ways To Inspire A Love Of Learning." Getting Smart blog. April 2015. http://gettingsmart.com/2015/04/10-ways-to-inspire-a-love-of-learning/

85. Binford, A. "Today's Busy Families Are Finding Time To Gather Around the Dinner Table." Getting Smart blog. April 2015. http://gettingsmart.com/2015/04/todays-busy-families-are-finding-time-to-gather-around-the-dinner-table/

86. Weiss, J. "Why Letting Youth Run the Store is Important for Their Development and Life Success." Getting Smart blog. June 2015. http://gettingsmart.com/2015/06/why-letting-youth-run-the-store-is-important-for-their-development-life-success/

87. Slusser, J. "Why Online Learning Works for Parents and Kids." June 2015. http://gettingsmart.com/2015/06/why-online-learning-works-for-parents-and-kids/

88. Connections Academy. "Annual Survey Results Reveal Why K-12 Students Attend Virtual Public Schools; Indicate Strong

Satisfaction." http://www.multivu.com/players/English/7310553-connections-education-satisfaction-survey/

89. Eames, J. "The 16 year old coder: Why My Daughter No Longer Attends Public High School." Getting Smart blog. January 2015. http://gettingsmart.com/2015/01/16-year-old-coder-daughter-no-longer-attends-public-high-school/

90. Iles, C. "Don't Let a Piece of Paper Place Children in an Educational Box." Getting Smart blog. January 2015. http://gettingsmart.com/2015/01/dont-let-piece-paper-place-children-educational-box/

91. Silverman, M. and Wilkes, S. "One Family's Journey Exemplifies Anytime-Anywhere Learning." Getting Smart blog. May 2015. http://gettingsmart.com/2015/05/one-familys-journey-exemplifies-anytime-anywhere-learning/

92. Schneider, C. "3 Ways Parents Can Spot Student-Centered Learning." Getting Smart blog. February 2015. http://gettingsmart.com/2015/02/3-ways-parents-can-spot-student-centered-learning/

93. Hosford, G. "Do Your Kids Need to Learn to Code? YES! But Not for the Reasons You Think." Getting Smart blog. May 2015. http://gettingsmart.com/2015/05/do-your-kids-need-to-learn-to-code-yes-but-not-for-the-reasons-you-think/

94. Watkins, C. "Learners in the driving seat." www.teachingtimes.com, http://www.ioe.ac.uk/about/documents/Watkins_09_lnr-driven.pdf

95. Bray, B. and McClaskey, K. Making Learning Personal: The What, Who, Wow, Where and Why. p. 11.

96. Bray, B. "Learning is Personal for Your Child." Getting Smart blog. June 2015. http://gettingsmart.com/2015/06/learning-is-personal-for-your-child/

97. Pew Research Center. http://www.pewsocialtrends.org/2014/02/11/the-rising-cost-of-not-going-to-college/

98. Northeastern University. "Innovation Imperative Series." http://www.northeastern.edu/innovationsurvey/

99. Vander Ark, T. "The Quest for an AA Degree in High School.'" Getting Smart blog. January 2015. http://gettingsmart.com/2015/01/quest-aa-degree-high-school/

100. Vander Ark, T. "Most Likely to Succeed: A Film About What School Could Be." Getting Smart blog. March 2015. See movie review at http://gettingsmart.com/2015/03/likely-succeed-film-school/

101. Vander Ark, T. "High Tech High: Student Engagement Leads

to Deeper Learning." Getting Smart blog. October 2013. http://gettingsmart.com/2013/10/high-tech-high-student-engagement-leads-deeper-learning/

102. Harlow, M. "If Ever There Was a Kid Born to Read." Getting Smart blog. February 2015. http://gettingsmart.com/2015/02/ever-kid-born-read/

103. Schneider, C. "What If We Replaced Family (and Classroom) Rules with Core Beliefs?" Getting Smart blog. February 2015. http://gettingsmart.com/2015/02/replaced-family-classroom-rules-core-beliefs/

104. Young, G. "Power of Play: Applied Knowledge, Engaged Learning." Getting Smart blog. April 2015. http://gettingsmart.com/2015/04/power-of-play-applied-knowledge-engaged-learning/

105. Althoff, E. "Pianist Seymour Bernstein teaches documentarian Ethan Hawke how to 'touch the sky.'" March 24, 2015. The Washington Times. http://www.washingtontimes.com/news/2015/mar/24/seymour-bernstein-piano-prodigy-and-teacher-featur/?page=all

106. "And the Quality Most Parents Want to Teach Their Children Is ..." Time. September 18, 2014. http://time.com/3393652/pew-research-parenting-american-trends/

107. Jeynes, W. "Parental Involvement and Student Achievement: A Meta-Analysis." Harvard Family Research Project. December 2005. http://www.hfrp.org/publications-resources/browse-our-publications/parental-involvement-and-student-achievement-a-meta-analysis

108. "Parental Involvement in Schools." Child Trends Data Bank. http://www.childtrends.org/?indicators=parental-involvement-in-schools

109. Walker, T. "America Closed the Opportunity Gap Once and 'We Can Do It Again', Says 'Our Kids' Author." NEA Today. May 18, 2015. http://neatoday.org/2015/05/18/america-closed-the-opportunity-gap-once-and-we-can-do-it-again-says-our-kids-author/?utm_source=150610neatodayexpress&utm_medium=email&utm_content=opp_agenda&utm_campaign=neatodayexpress

110. Perry, K. "Early Childhood Education is Critical for our Own Kids' Future – and the Nation's." Getting Smart blog. March 2015. http://gettingsmart.com/2015/03/early-childhood-education-is-critical-for-our-own-kids-future-and-the-nations/

111. Ibid.

112. Guernsey, L. "Common Sense, Science-Based Advice on Early

Learners' Screen Time." Getting Smart blog. February 2015. http://gettingsmart.com/2015/02/common-sense-science-based-advice-early-learners-screen-time/

113. Staker, H. "How to Keep Children From Drowning in the Device Deep End." Getting Smart blog. April 2015. http://gettingsmart.com/2015/04/how-to-keep-children-from-drowning-in-the-device-deep-end/

114. Miller, M. "How to Turn Screen Time into Family Time." Getting Smart blog. March 2015. http://gettingsmart.com/2015/03/how-to-turn-screen-time-into-family-time/

115. Wimmer, L. "The Elementary School Years: The Four Pillars That Build a Strong Foundation." Getting Smart blog. August 2015. http://gettingsmart.com/the-elementary-years-four-pillars-that-build-a-strong-foundation

116. Briceño, E. "Growth Mindset Parenting." Getting Smart blog. March 2015. http://gettingsmart.com/2015/03/growth-mindset-parenting/

117. Ryerse, M. "You Can Thank Mom for More than the Meal Itself: Family Dinner Matters." Getting Smart blog. May 2015. http://gettingsmart.com/2015/05/you-can-thank-mom-for-more-than-the-meal-itself-family-dinner-matters/

118. Mead, M. "Understanding Your Middle Schooler: 4 Tips for Success." Getting Smart blog. August 2015. http://gettingsmart.com/2015/07/understanding-your-middle-schooler-4-tips-for-success/

119. Wyatt-Ross, J. "Kids, Smart Phones, and Social Media: 6 Rules for Success and Safety." Getting Smart blog. March 2015. http://gettingsmart.com/2015/03/kids-smart-phones-and-social-media-6-rules-for-success-and-safety/

120. Thorpe, C. "The Power of Personal Relationship in Personalized Learning." Getting Smart blog. March 2015. http://gettingsmart.com/2015/03/power-personal-relationship-personalized-learning/

121. Silverman, M. and Wilkes, S. "One Family's Journey Exemplifies Anytime-Anywhere Learning." Getting Smart blog. May 2015. http://gettingsmart.com/2015/05/one-familys-journey-exemplifies-anytime-anywhere-learning/

122. Vander Ark, T. "Parenting for Powerful Learning: 35 Tips." Getting Smart blog. March 2015. http://gettingsmart.com/2015/03/parenting-for-powerful-learning-35-tips/

123. Jensen, Dr. F. "The Teenage Brain: Scaffolding the Brain

for Lifelong Learning." Getting Smart blog. May 2015. http:// gettingsmart.com/2015/05/the-teenage-brain-scaffolding-the-brain-for-lifelong-learning/

124. Barash, C. "10 Things Parents of High School Juniors Should Start Doing Now." Getting Smart blog. March 2015. http:// gettingsmart.com/2015/03/10-things-parents-of-high-school-juniors-should-start-doing-now/

125. Ferguson, R. "Sage Advice from a Higher Ed Veteran: Getting a Head Start on Finding the Right College." Getting Smart blog. August 2015. http://gettingsmart.com/2015/08/ sage-advice-from-a-higher-ed-veteran-getting-a-head-start-on-finding-the-right-college/

126. Vander Ark, T. "Parenting for Powerful Learning: 35 Tips." Getting Smart blog. March 2015. http://gettingsmart.com/2015/03/ parenting-for-powerful-learning-35-tips/

127. Lathram, B. "8 Noncognitive Competencies for College and Career Readiness." Getting Smart blog. February 2015. http:// gettingsmart.com/2015/02/8-non-cognitive-competencies-college-career-readiness/

128. Frank, A., and Waidelich, K. "Doctor, Lawyer, Camel Rancher? Helping Your Kids Discover Careers They Love." Getting Smart blog. February 2015. http://gettingsmart.com/2015/02/doctor-lawyer-camel-rancher-helping-kids-discover-careers-love/

129. Vander Ark, T. "Your Kid Just Said He's Not Going to College, Now What?" Getting Smart blog. May 2015. http://gettingsmart. com/2015/06/your-kid-just-said-hes-not-going-to-college-now-what/

130. Lathram, B. "Is Your Child's School Student-Centered? A Checklist for School Visits." Getting Smart blog. March 2015. http:// gettingsmart.com/2015/03/is-your-childs-school-student-centered-a-checklist-for-school-visits/

131. Lathram, B. "Learning Plans: The What, When, Why and How to Do Them Well." Getting Smart blog. June 2015. http://gettingsmart. com/2015/06/learning-plans-the-what-when-why-and-how-to-do-them-well-2/

132. Gruber, G. "Your Child, Your Choice: Finding the Right School for Your Child." Getting Smart blog. June 2015. http:// gettingsmart.com/2015/06/your-child-your-choice-finding-the-right-school-for-your-child/

133. Miller, J. "The Power of Parenting with Social and Emotional Learning." Getting Smart blog. April 2015. http://gettingsmart. com/2015/04/the-power-of-parenting-with-social-and-emotional-learning/

134. Bray, B. "Learning is Personal for Your Child." Getting Smart blog. June 2015. http://gettingsmart.com/2015/06/learning-is-personal-for-your-child/

135. Schneider, C. "10 Ways To Inspire A Love Of Learning." Getting Smart blog. April 2015. http://gettingsmart.com/2015/04/10-ways-to-inspire-a-love-of-learning/

136. Weinstein, N. "Parents as Chief Advocates." Getting Smart blog. March 2015. http://gettingsmart.com/2015/03/parents-as-chief-advocates/

137. Ryerse, M. "Lessons for Learning and Life: 10 Messages Parents (and Teachers) Can Teach Kids. Getting Smart blog. February 2015. http://gettingsmart.com/2015/02/lessons-learning-life-10-messages-parents-teachers-can-teach-kids/

138. Makhani, R. "10 Strategies to Help Children Define Success for Themselves." Getting Smart blog. April 2015. http://gettingsmart.com/2015/04/10-strategies-to-help-children-define-success-for-themselves/

139. Sampson, Dr. S. "How To Raise A Wild Child: The Art And Science Of Falling In Love With Nature." Getting Smart blog. April 2015. http://gettingsmart.com/2015/04/how-to-raise-a-wild-child-the-art-and-science-of-falling-in-love-with-nature/

Digital Edition

To receive your non-transferable digital
edition of this book, please visit
www.eifrigpublishing.com/getting-smart
and follow the instructions provided.

23487371R00189

Made in the USA
San Bernardino, CA
20 August 2015